SIMPLY ELEGANT

A
Celebration of
Good Living and Good Taste

SIMPLY ELEGANT

The Cuisine of the Windsor Court Hotel

KEVIN GRAHAM

Photographs by Jerry Simpson

GROVE WEIDENFELD NEW YORK

Published by Grove Weidenfeld
A division of Grove Press, Inc.
841 Broadway
New York, NY   10003-4793

Published in Canada by General Publishing Company, Ltd.

Library of Congress Cataloging-in-Publication Data

Graham, Kevin.
    Simply elegant : the cuisine of the Windsor Court Hotel / Kevin
Graham.
       p.   cm.
    Includes index.
    ISBN 0-8021-1297-8 : $25.00
    1. Cookery.   2. Windsor Court Hotel (New Orleans, La.). Grill
Room.   I. Title.
TX714.G74   1991
641.5—dc20   90-26043
                                                         CIP

Manufactured in the United States of America

Printed on acid-free paper

Designed by Irving Perkins Associates

First Edition 1991

10   9   8   7   6   5   4   3   2   1

Acknowledgments

I would like to thank my wife, Suzy, and my children, Katie and Alexis, for their ongoing support as I pursue my goals. To Jean Mestriner, for his remarkable leadership and trust, which continually inspired me and influenced Windsor Court to become the world-class hotel it is today.

To Bill, Jeff, and Harvey, who personally ensured that daily responsibilities were carried out. To the many culinary testers, for their time and comments, which assisted in the development of my recipes.

I found a new friend in Jerry Simpson, whose extraordinary photography exemplified my work—and he really does look like John Lennon.

Lastly, I would like to thank all the others whose efforts were involved in the production of this book.

CONTENTS

From the Executive Office   *ix*

A Celebration of Good Taste   *xi*

I   Soups   *1*

II   Salads and Dressings   *15*

III   Appetizers   *31*

IV   Pastas   *67*

V   Fish and Shellfish   *81*

VI   Fowl   *107*

VII   Game   *125*

VIII   Meats   *135*

IX   Side Dishes and Vegetables   *151*

X   Sauces and Stocks   *167*

XI   Breakfast and Brunch   *191*

XII   Desserts   *211*

Index   *245*

From the Executive Office

The location of the Windsor Court Hotel, adjacent to the Mississippi River, is no coincidence. The river is, and always has been, the focal point for the city, assuring New Orleans its global reputation. Its commerce and vitality assert international influence and serve as a welcome to visitors from all over the world.

Prior to 1984 and the opening of Windsor Court, no hotel existed in New Orleans that equaled the magnetism of the city, able to completely serve the diverse needs of sophisticated world travelers. The great hotels of Europe developed from a long tradition of grand service and luxurious hospitality. The developer of Windsor Court, distinguished New Orleanian James J. Coleman, Jr., recognized this, and it was his dream to instill in his hotel such a tradition. For this reason, Windsor Court's decor encompasses fine English paintings, sculptures, tapestries, and furnishings dating from the seventeenth century, recalling an English country home with generations of careful collecting.

Here at Windsor Court, we recognized that the heart and

soul of a great hotel is the food, wine, and service, and he had a constant dedication to quality. The Grill Room is rated one of the top fifteen restaurants in the country by several independent sources, and our twelve-thousand-bottle wine cellar is one of the best in the region.

Because of this vision we are able to administer Windsor Court the way most hoteliers dream about running a hotel—the best way possible. Windsor Court's great success and dedicated following prove this. The hotel continues to be named to the "Top Ten Hotels" lists for both the United States and the world, and garners such top honors as the American Automobile Association's five-diamond rating each year.

The unique Windsor Court style is evident everywhere, not only in the Grill Room. It shows in the attention to details: the warm welcome from our doorman after a long flight, or the way our concierge remembers your favorite restaurant and our rooms attendants make you feel comfortably at home. This style keeps us on the cutting edge, constantly improving our facilities and services to give our discriminating guests the best quality available.

Ours is a stewardship we will pass on to the next manager, the next executive chef, after taking Windsor Court as far as we can. The success of the Windsor Court Hotel today is the result of an infusion of progressive ideas. Chef Kevin Graham has written this book to share these ideas with you as a souvenir of the great tradition we build here each day—a true celebration of good taste and good living.

JEAN V. MESTRINER
Executive Vice President
Managing Director

A Celebration of Good Taste

A luxury hotel is most fully realized in its dining room, and the Grill Room of the Windsor Court Hotel is no exception. Here I have had the opportunity to create a *grande cuisine* for an elegant room recalling the luxury of dining in a bygone era. This timeless quality and the unerring support of New Orleanians have enabled us to begin a great culinary tradition, not simply create a passing food trend.

The food that you find in this book is diverse, reflecting the various cuisines that inspire me as well as my daily exploration of products from the world market. I have tried to offer in my recipes the many flavors of Windsor Court. This does not mean that the dishes found here will be seen on a daily basis, as the Grill Room menus are revised continually to reflect the availability of produce and to meet the seasonal needs of our clients. For instance, the hearty Wild Fowl Braised with Port is ideally suited for the winter, while Tuna with Two Sesames, Wasabi Beurre Blanc, and Shiitake Mushrooms, or Lobster Poached in Honeyed Water with Citrus Mayonnaise is perfect for lighter summer appetites.

Being foremost a New Orleans restaurant, the Grill Room also features the great dishes the city is known for, but with distinct Windsor Court accents. These dishes include Turtle Soup, Oyster-Artichoke Soup, Louisiana Crab Cakes with Fresh Tomato Tartar Sauce, and Traditional New Orleans Pralines, and all have quickly become Grill Room favorites, requested especially by New Orleanians.

Local products figure in many of our Grill Room dishes, and I am particularly taken by the bounty of Louisiana. For instance, the birds I use for Roasted Abita Springs Quail with Port-Coriander Sauce are grown on the farm of a friend of mine, and this particular dish reflects a combination of new- and old-world influences that continually inspire me. Other ingredients indigenous to the area that I utilize often in my kitchen are crawfish, shrimp, red snapper, Tabasco sauce, oysters, and Pontchatoula strawberries.

Being chef to a global clientele has spurred me to create dishes in a unique Windsor Court style in which there are no boundaries or nationalities. Borrowing from the great British favorite that uses shrimp, I have brought Potted Crawfish to the Grill Room. A variation on the classic New Orleans baked oyster dishes is Oysters Polo, originally created for our client Avanti Automobiles. Omelette Linley is a tribute to Viscount Linley, whose beautiful marquetry screens are the focal point of the Grill Room, and Eggs Windsor Court are a sensationally rich brunch item.

A disciplined approach based on the classical French cuisine of Escoffier is necessary to every great kitchen. Recognizing this, I created here the elegant Grilled Foie Gras and Pears, velvety Shrimp and Cilantro Bisque, and traditional Tournedos of Beef with Red Butter and Beef Marrow.

I have selected and written the recipes in this cookbook with much thought and admiration for the home cook. No recipe was included that could not be reproduced in the home kitchens of our testers. Moreover, in this book we bring to you the luxury of Windsor Court—where New Orleans brings the world to dine—so that you might entertain your family and friends as graciously and easily as we have ours.

Bon Appetit.

CHEF KEVIN GRAHAM
January 1991

I SOUPS

Shrimp and Cilantro Bisque

Oyster-Artichoke Soup

Crab and Corn Soup
   with Corn Fritters

Turtle Soup

Strawberry Champagne Soup

Chanterelle and Tomato Soup

Gazpacho
   with Cumin, Basil, and Crabmeat

Shrimp and Cilantro Bisque

SERVES 8

1½ pounds fresh shrimp
1½ sticks (¾ cup) unsalted butter
1 yellow onion, peeled and finely chopped
2 cloves garlic, peeled and finely chopped
4 stalks celery, trimmed and finely chopped
2 tablespoons tomato paste
4 tablespoons ground coriander
¼ teaspoon cayenne pepper

6 cups shrimp stock or Fish Stock (see page 170)
¼ cup white wine
¼ cup Madeira
3 medium-size baking potatoes, peeled and finely cubed
Salt to taste
Freshly ground white pepper to taste
1 cup heavy cream
½ cup finely chopped cilantro (or to taste)

Peel and devein the shrimp, reserving the heads (if attached) and shells. Dice the meat and set aside.

Melt the butter in a large saucepan over medium heat. Add the shrimp shells (and heads, if any) and stir for about 1 minute, or until pink. Remove the shells (and heads) with a slotted spoon, leaving the butter in the pan. Add the onion, garlic, and celery and sauté for 2 minutes, or until tender. Stir in the diced shrimp. When pink, add the tomato paste, coriander, and cayenne pepper. Simmer for 5 minutes, then add the shrimp stock, wine, Madeira, and potatoes. Raise the heat and bring to a rolling boil. Lower the heat and simmer for 20 minutes.

Strain the liquid into a clean saucepan. Place over medium heat and bring to a simmer. Lower the heat to a low simmer. Purée the shrimp and vegetables in a blender or food processor fitted with the metal blade. Add the purée to the simmering liquid, a tablespoon at a time, until the soup is thick enough to coat the back of a spoon. Season with salt and pepper. Stir in the heavy cream. Strain the soup once again, then fold in 1/4 cup cilantro.

Pour equal portions into each of eight warm soup bowls and garnish with a sprinkling of the remaining 1/4 cup cilantro. Serve immediately.

Oyster-Artichoke Soup

SERVES 6

1 stick (¹/₂ cup) unsalted
    butter
3 dozen oysters, shucked
1 bunch scallions, trimmed
    and chopped
2 stalks celery, trimmed and
    chopped
¹/₄ teaspoon dried thyme,
    crumbled
¹/₂ cup all-purpose flour

6 cups Fish Stock (see page 170)
1 cup heavy cream
6 artichoke hearts, quartered (if
    using canned artichoke hearts,
    rinse well and pat dry)
Salt to taste
Freshly ground white pepper
    to taste

Melt the butter in a large saucepan over medium heat. Add the oysters and sauté for 2 minutes, or just until the edges curl. Remove from the pan and set aside, keeping warm. Place the scallions, celery, and thyme in the pan and sauté for 4 minutes, or until soft but not browned. Add the flour and cook for 3 to 4 minutes, or until well blended. Slowly whisk in the fish stock and cream. Bring to a simmer, then cover and simmer for 30 minutes.

Add the artichoke hearts, season with salt and pepper, and simmer for an additional 5 minutes. Just before serving, add the warm oysters. Transfer to a tureen and serve immediately.

Crab and Corn Soup with Corn Fritters

SERVES 8

6 ears fresh yellow corn (to yield 3 cups kernels)
1/4 cup Clarified Butter (see page 180)
1/2 yellow onion, peeled and finely chopped
1 clove garlic, peeled and finely chopped
1/8 teaspoon dried thyme, crumbled
1/2 cup all-purpose flour

4 cups hot Fish Stock (see page 170)
2 cups heavy cream
1/2 pound fresh lump crabmeat, picked over to remove any shell and cartilage
Salt to taste
Freshly ground white pepper to taste
Corn Fritters (see recipe below)

Shuck the corn. Remove all silk and cut the raw kernels from the cob. Set aside.

Heat the butter in a large heavy pot over medium heat. Add the onion, garlic, and thyme and sauté for 2 minutes, or until the onion is soft but not browned. Stir in the corn kernels and cook for 5 minutes. Sprinkle the flour over the vegetable mixture, stirring until well blended. Gradually whisk the hot fish stock into the mixture. When the soup is smooth, add the cream and crabmeat. Lower the heat and simmer for about 15 minutes, or until the amount of liquid is reduced by one third. Season with salt and pepper. Transfer to a tureen and serve hot. Pass the Corn Fritters on the side.

Corn Fritters
MAKES 16

1 cup freshly scraped corn kernels (canned cream-style corn may be substituted)
1/2 cup all-purpose flour

3 large egg yolks, well beaten
1 teaspoon dried marjoram
1/4 teaspoon salt
Vegetable oil for frying

If using fresh corn, use a potato masher to crush the corn kernels. Combine with the flour, egg yolks, marjoram, and salt. Stir to blend.

Pour 1/4 inch of oil into a small skillet and heat over medium-high heat. Drop tablespoons of batter into the pan and fry for 2 minutes, or until golden brown. Turn and brown the other side. Cook in batches, adding more oil to the pan as necessary. Drain on paper towels and serve immediately with Crab and Corn Soup.

Turtle Soup

1 pound turtle meat, cut into pieces (1 pound veal shank may be substituted, to make Mock Turtle Soup)
1/2 pound lean veal, cut into pieces
3 yellow onions, peeled
2 bay leaves
1 whole clove
Salt
1/4 cup peanut oil
1 green bell pepper, stemmed, seeded, and finely chopped
4 stalks celery, trimmed and chopped

2 tomatoes, peeled, seeded, and chopped
Freshly ground black pepper
1/2 teaspoon cayenne pepper
1 teaspoon dried thyme
1 teaspoon rubbed sage
6 cups Chicken Stock (see page 169)
1 cup dry sherry
1/4 cup finely chopped parsley
2 hard-boiled eggs, finely chopped
1 lemon, thinly sliced and seeds removed

Thoroughly wash the turtle meat under cold running water. Place the turtle meat, veal, 1 whole onion, the bay leaves, clove, a pinch of salt, and 4 quarts of water in a stock pot over medium heat. Bring to a boil, skimming any scum that forms on the surface. Lower the heat and simmer, uncovered, for 2 hours. Remove from the heat and let cool at room temperature.

Finely chop the remaining onions. Heat the oil in a large saucepan over medium heat. Add the chopped onions, green pepper, celery, and tomatoes and sauté for 2 minutes, or until the onions are tender. Add ½ teaspoon black pepper and the cayenne, thyme, and sage. Stir in the chicken stock and remove from the heat.

With a slotted spoon, remove the turtle and veal meat from their stock. Set aside. Return the stock to high heat and boil for 20 minutes, or until the liquid is reduced to 4 cups. Finely dice the turtle and veal meat (or pass it through a medium grinder). Add the meat to the chicken stock. Strain the reduced turtle stock into the pot. Return to high heat and bring to a rolling boil. Lower the heat to medium-high and cook, uncovered, for 30 minutes. Adjust the seasoning with salt and pepper.

Just before serving, pour the soup into a tureen and stir in ½ cup sherry, the parsley, eggs, and lemon slices. Pass the remaining ½ cup sherry at the table.

Strawberry Champagne Soup

SERVES 4

2 pints fresh ripe strawberries, chilled
1/2 cup freshly squeezed orange juice
1/4 cup honey

1/4 cup green chartreuse liqueur
1/2 bottle dry champagne, chilled
10 mint leaves, shredded

Place four glass serving bowls in the freezer to chill.

Wash the strawberries and blot dry. Remove the stems. Place in a blender or food processor fitted with the metal blade and purée with the orange juice. Combine the honey and the chartreuse in a saucepan over high heat. Bring to a quick boil. Immediately remove from the heat and transfer to a large bowl. Fold in the strawberry purée, cover, and refrigerate.

When the mixture is thoroughly chilled, add the champagne and spoon equal portions into the four chilled bowls. Garnish with the shredded mint leaves and serve immediately.

Chanterelle and Tomato Soup

SERVES 6

4 ounces chanterelle
    mushrooms (any fresh
    mushrooms may be
    substituted)
1/2 stick (1/4 cup) unsalted
    butter
1 yellow onion, peeled and
    finely chopped
2 cloves garlic, peeled and
    finely chopped
1/4 cup plus 2 tablespoons all-
    purpose flour
41/2 cups Chicken Stock (see
    page 169)
11/2 cups heavy cream
    Salt to taste
    Freshly ground white
    pepper to taste

1/4 cup Clarified Butter (see
    page 180) or vegetable oil
2 slices raw bacon, chopped
1 bay leaf
    Pinch of dried basil
1 medium carrot, peeled and
    chopped
2 stalks celery, trimmed and
    chopped
1/2 cup tomato paste
2 very ripe tomatoes, seeded
    and chopped (2 cups drained,
    chopped canned tomatoes
    may be substituted)
2 tablespoons sugar
2 tablespoons cider vinegar

Wash the mushrooms. Drain on paper towels and pat dry. Cut
into thin slices. Melt the unsalted butter in a medium saucepan
over high heat. Add the mushrooms, half the onion, and half
the garlic. Lower the heat and sauté for 2 minutes, or until the

onion is tender. Stir in ¼ cup flour until well blended. Add 2 cups chicken stock, stirring until smooth. Lower the heat and simmer for 10 minutes, stirring occasionally. Remove the pan from the heat and whisk in 1 cup cream. Transfer to a blender or food processor fitted with the metal blade and purée for about 30 seconds, or until smooth. Return to the heat just to warm. Season with salt and pepper and keep warm.

Heat the clarified butter in a heavy pan over medium heat. Add the bacon, the remaining onion and garlic, the bay leaf, basil, carrot, and celery and sauté for 2 minutes, or until the vegetables are tender. Add the tomato paste and cook, stirring constantly, for 2 to 3 minutes. Stir in the remaining 2 table-spoons flour and the tomatoes. When well blended, whisk in the remaining 2½ cups chicken stock. Simmer for 25 minutes. Remove from the heat. Pick out the bay leaf and stir in the remaining ½ cup cream.

Place the mixture in a blender or food processor fitted with the metal blade and purée until smooth. Strain the soup into a clean saucepan. Return to low heat.

Heat the sugar in a small skillet over low heat. Cook for about 4 minutes, or until caramelized. Stir in the vinegar until the sugar is dissolved. Add to the tomato soup, a bit at a time, according to taste.

Using two ladles at the same time, pour equal portions of each soup into six flat, warm soup bowls so that the soups meet in the center but do not blend. Serve immediately.

Gazpacho with Cumin, Basil, and Crabmeat

SERVES 4

4 tomatoes, peeled, seeded, and
  quartered
2 cloves garlic, peeled and
  crushed
1 small cucumber, peeled,
  seeded, and quartered
1/2 yellow onion, peeled and
  quartered
1 green bell pepper, stemmed,
  seeded, and quartered
  Pinch of cayenne pepper
  Pinch of cumin
1 teaspoon rice wine vinegar

3 tablespoons olive oil
  Salt to taste
  Freshly ground white pepper
  to taste
1/2 pound fresh lump crabmeat,
  picked over to remove any
  shell and cartilage
1 teaspoon minced fresh basil
1 small baguette French bread
  (optional)
4 cloves garlic, peeled and cut
  in half (optional)
  Additional olive oil (optional)

Place the tomatoes, garlic, cucumber, onion, green pepper, cayenne pepper, cumin, vinegar, and oil in a blender or food processor fitted with the metal blade and purée on high speed for 1 minute, or until the mixture reaches the consistency of tomato soup. Season with salt and pepper, cover, and chill in the refrigerator for at least 1 hour.

Place four glass serving bowls in the freezer to chill.

Refrigerate the crabmeat until ready to use.

When the gazpacho is thoroughly chilled, remove from the refrigerator and stir well. Pour equal portions into the four chilled bowls. Spoon an equal portion of crabmeat into the center of each and sprinkle with the minced basil. Serve immediately.

If desired as an accompaniment, cut the French bread into slices ½ inch thick and toast. Rub one side of the toasted slices with the garlic halves and drizzle with olive oil. Serve immediately with the chilled soup.

II

SALADS AND DRESSINGS

Windsor Court Salad
with Sauce Lorenzo

Spinach Salad
with Hot Crabmeat Dressing

Baby Lettuces
with Lemon Parmesan Vinaigrette

Lamb's Lettuce Salad
with Celery and Pink Peppercorn Dressing

Shredded Spinach Salad
with Sugared Toasted Almonds and Creamy Vinaigrette

Cucumber Salad

Hot Crawfish
with Gingered Sesame on Watercress

Creole Tomato Salad

Fresh Herb Cheese
with Endive and Bibb Lettuce

Windsor Court Salad with Sauce Lorenzo

SERVES 8 TO 10

1 head romaine lettuce, separated, rinsed, and dried
2 bunches watercress, stemmed, thoroughly rinsed in salted water, and dried
2 large hard-boiled eggs, whites and yolks separated
6 radishes, rinsed and trimmed

2 ounces Roquefort cheese
2 large tomatoes, peeled and cored
4 slices cooked bacon
1 large avocado, peeled and pit removed
Sauce Lorenzo (see recipe below)

Finely chop all the ingredients, one at a time, and arrange side by side in a large salad bowl. Just before serving, toss with Sauce Lorenzo. Serve immediately.

Sauce Lorenzo

MAKES 2 CUPS

1 large egg yolk
1 teaspoon Dijon mustard
1 cup vegetable oil
$^{1}/_{3}$ cup red wine vinegar
1 shallot, peeled and chopped

2 tablespoons bottled chili sauce
Salt to taste
Freshly ground black pepper to taste

Lightly beat together the egg yolk and mustard. Alternately, add the oil and vinegar in a steady stream, whisking rapidly to emulsify. Stir in the chopped shallot and chili sauce. Season with salt and pepper.

Sauce Lorenzo may be stored, covered, in the refrigerator for up to 3 months.

Spinach Salad with Hot Crabmeat Dressing

SERVES 4

¹/₂ cup olive oil
2 shallots, peeled and finely chopped
2 cloves garlic, peeled and finely chopped
2 teaspoons Dijon mustard
¹/₄ cup rice wine vinegar
Pinch of cayenne pepper
Salt to taste
Freshly ground black pepper to taste

4 ounces fresh lump crabmeat, picked over to remove any shell and cartilage
6 ounces fresh spinach, stemmed, thoroughly rinsed in salted water, and dried
1 tomato, peeled, seeded, and thinly sliced
3 fresh mushrooms, stemmed, cleaned, and thinly sliced

Heat the oil in a small saucepan over medium heat. Add the shallots and garlic and sauté for 2 minutes, or until tender. Whisk in the mustard, vinegar, and cayenne. Season with salt and black pepper, then fold in the crabmeat. Cook for a few seconds to warm through.

Break the spinach into bite-size pieces and place in a serving bowl. Pour the crabmeat dressing over the spinach and toss to coat. Place an equal portion on each of four salad plates and garnish with the tomato and mushroom slices. Serve immediately.

Baby Lettuces with
Lemon Parmesan Vinaigrette

SERVES 4

¹/₂ cup vegetable oil
1 large egg yolk
1 teaspoon Creole mustard or other grainy mustard
2 tablespoons champagne vinegar or white wine vinegar
2–4 tablespoons freshly squeezed lemon juice
Dash of Tabasco sauce
¹/₂ teaspoon freshly ground black pepper
¹/₂ teaspoon grated fresh lemon zest

¹/₄ cup freshly grated Parmesan cheese
¹/₂ bunch baby red oak lettuce, separated, rinsed, and dried
¹/₂ bunch baby green oak lettuce, separated, rinsed, and dried
¹/₂ head baby romaine lettuce, separated, rinsed, and dried
¹/₂ head Kentucky limestone Bibb lettuce, separated, rinsed, and dried (any soft-leaf lettuce may be substituted)

Whisk the oil, egg yolk, and mustard together in a mixing bowl. When well combined, slowly incorporate the vinegar and lemon juice. Whisk in the Tabasco, pepper, lemon zest, and Parmesan cheese. Let sit at room temperature for 2 hours. (If not used after 2 hours, cover and refrigerate.)

Place the lettuce leaves in a salad bowl, drizzle the vinaigrette on top, and toss lightly. Serve immediately.

Lamb's Lettuce Salad with Celery and Pink Peppercorn Dressing

SERVES 4

²/₃ cup rice wine vinegar
2 tablespoons dried pink peppercorns
1¹/₂ cups peanut oil
4 teaspoons minced shallots
4 stalks celery, trimmed and finely chopped

1 tablespoon Dijon mustard
Salt to taste
Freshly ground black pepper to taste
8 ounces lamb's lettuce (mâche), separated, thoroughly rinsed, and dried

Combine the vinegar and pink peppercorns in a saucepan over medium heat. Bring to a simmer and cook for 2 minutes, or until the peppercorns are soft. Remove from the heat and cool to room temperature.

In a blender, combine the vinegar and peppercorns with the oil, shallots, celery, and mustard. When blended thoroughly, season with salt and pepper. Place the lettuce in a salad bowl, drizzle the vinaigrette on top, and toss lightly. Serve immediately.

Any leftover dressing may be stored, covered, in the refrigerator for up to 3 months.

Shredded Spinach Salad with Sugared Toasted Almonds and Creamy Vinaigrette

SERVES 4

¹/₂ pound fresh spinach
¹/₂ cup slivered almonds,
blanched
2 tablespoons confectioners'
sugar

Creamy Vinaigrette (see
recipe below)

Remove the stems from the spinach leaves and rinse the leaves in salted water three times to remove any grit. Rinse under cold running water. Dry thoroughly.

Preheat the broiler.

Using a sharp knife, cut the spinach into a chiffonade (a very fine julienne). Divide equally among four salad plates. Refrigerate.

Place the almonds on a baking sheet and place under the preheated broiler. Toast for 1 minute, or until golden brown. Remove from the oven and dust with the confectioners' sugar.

Sprinkle an equal portion of almonds on each plate of

spinach, then drizzle the Creamy Vinaigrette on top. Serve immediately.

Creamy Vinaigrette
MAKES 1¼ CUPS

1 large egg yolk
¼ teaspoon Dijon mustard or whole-grain mustard
1 tablespoon freshly squeezed lemon juice

¼ teaspoon salt
¼ teaspoon freshly ground black pepper
¾ cup peanut oil
3 tablespoons red wine vinegar

In a blender, combine the egg yolk, mustard, lemon juice, salt, and pepper.

When well combined, with the motor running, incorporate separately half of the oil and half of the vinegar in thin streams until emulsified. Gradually add the remaining oil and vinegar, alternately, until thoroughly blended.

Any leftover dressing may be stored, covered, in the refrigerator for up to 3 months.

Cucumber Salad

SERVES 4

1 pound European or hothouse cucumbers, peeled, seeded, and thinly sliced (any burpless cucumber may be substituted)
1 tablespoon salt

8 mint leaves, cut into a chiffonade (a very fine julienne)
¹/₄ cup Creamy Vinaigrette (see page 23)

Combine the cucumber slices and salt in a bowl. Let sit at room temperature for 20 minutes, then place the cucumber in a colander and rinse thoroughly under cold running water. Drain and pat dry.

Place the well-dried cucumber in a clean bowl and toss with the mint leaves. Cover and chill for at least 1 hour. Just before serving, toss with the Creamy Vinaigrette. Serve immediately.

Serve as an accompaniment to Pâté of Salmon and Crabmeat en Croûte (see page 46), or other seafood dishes.

Hot Crawfish with
Gingered Sesame on Watercress

SERVES 4

2 bunches fresh watercress,
   stemmed
¹/₄ cup sugar
¹/₄ cup peeled and finely
   chopped fresh gingerroot
¹/₄ cup rice wine vinegar
¹/₄ cup Stone's Green Ginger
   Wine (dry sherry may be
   substituted)

¹/₄ cup peanut oil or vegetable
   oil
2 tablespoons chopped shallots
1 pound cooked crawfish tail
   meat
Salt to taste
Freshly ground black pepper
   to taste

Rinse the watercress thoroughly in salted water. Drain until
dry. Divide the leaves equally among four salad plates. Refrigerate until ready to serve.

Place the sugar in a heavy skillet over medium heat. Cook for
about 4 minutes, or until the sugar dissolves and turns a light
brown color, being careful not to burn. Add the ginger, vinegar,
and ginger wine and stir until the caramelized sugar is completely dissolved. Cook for about 5 minutes, or until the liquid
is reduced by half.

Heat the oil in a separate pan over medium heat. Add the shallots and sauté for about 2 minutes, or until soft. Add the crawfish meat and the ginger mixture. Raise the heat and, stirring constantly, cook for 1 minute, or until heated through. Do not overcook. Season with salt and pepper. Spoon equal portions over the plates of watercress and serve immediately.

Creole Tomato Salad

SERVES 4

4 large, very ripe Creole
  tomatoes, cored and
  quartered (any ripe vine
  tomatoes may be substituted)
1/4 red onion, peeled
2 cloves garlic, peeled
4 leaves fresh basil
2/3 cup olive oil
1/3 cup champagne vinegar or
  apple cider vinegar

1/4 teaspoon freshly ground
  black pepper
1/4 teaspoon Tabasco sauce
1/4 teaspoon salt
1 head romaine lettuce,
  separated, rinsed, and dried
2 tablespoons grated Romano
  cheese

Place four salad plates in the freezer to chill.

Place all the ingredients except the lettuce and Romano cheese in a blender or food processor fitted with the metal blade. Blend at high speed for 30 seconds.

Break the romaine into bite-size pieces and divide equally among the four chilled plates. Pour 2 tablespoons dressing over each serving and sprinkle with Romano cheese. Serve immediately.

Any leftover Creole tomato dressing may be stored, covered, in the refrigerator for up to 2 weeks.

Fresh Herb Cheese with Endive and Bibb Lettuce

SERVES 4

½ gallon milk
¼ cup freshly squeezed lemon juice
⅜ teaspoon salt
⅛ teaspoon freshly ground white pepper
1 tablespoon snipped fresh chives (chopped fresh basil may be substituted)

2 heads Belgian endive, separated, rinsed, and dried
2 heads Bibb lettuce, separated, rinsed, and dried
¼ cup olive oil

Place the milk in a deep heavy saucepan over high heat. Heat almost to a boil. Stir, gently scraping the bottom and sides of the pan, to prevent sticking. Remove from the heat and with a rubber spatula, slowly stir in the lemon juice. The milk will turn greenish in color and begin to curdle. Cover the pan and let sit 15 minutes at room temperature.

Line a sieve or colander with three layers of cheesecloth and pour the curdled milk through. Drain 10 to 15 minutes. Gently fold the salt, pepper, and chives into the curds. Gather the edges of the cheesecloth like a bag, tie the top, and hang over a bowl for 1 hour, or until the curds are completely drained and firm.

Place the cheesecloth bag in a bowl or mold just large enough to hold it tightly. Cover with a plate weighted with a 1-pound weight. Refrigerate for at least 8 hours.

Place four salad plates in the freezer to chill.

When the cheese is firm, unmold and peel away the cheesecloth. Break the endive and lettuce leaves into bite-size pieces and toss in a bowl to combine. Divide equally among the four chilled plates. Crumble the cheese over the top of the salads and drizzle with the olive oil. Serve immediately.

III

APPETIZERS

Crawfish Sarah Jane

Crawfish Sausage

Potted Crawfish

Oysters Polo

Shrimp Sautéed with Citrus Fruit

Rillettes of Lobster and Avocado
with Cilantro Yogurt Sauce

Crabmeat Soufflé

Pâté of Salmon and Crabmeat en Croûte

Quenelles of Seafood
with Tarragon Cream Sauce

Smoked Redfish
with Cucumber Jam

Sautéed Snails
with Folsom Chanterelles

Fried Frog's Legs
with Champagne Mustard Sauce

Beggar's Purses
with Caviar

Grilled Foie Gras and Pears

Terrine of Chicken and Goose Livers
with Cumberland Sauce

Confit of Duck Legs and Lentils

Steak Romanoff

Crawfish Sarah Jane

SERVES 4

6 tablespoons unsalted butter
1/2 pound cooked crawfish tail
  meat
2 tablespoons finely chopped
  shallots
2 tablespoons freshly squeezed
  lime juice

1/4 cup tequila
  Pinch of cayenne pepper
1/2 cup heavy cream
  Salt to taste
  Freshly ground white pepper
  to taste
4 wedges lime, dipped in salt

Melt 2 tablespoons butter in a medium sauté pan over medium-high heat. Add the crawfish meat and sauté for 1 minute. Remove with a slotted spoon and reserve. Add the shallots to the pan and sauté for 2 minutes, or until tender. Add the lime juice, tequila, and cayenne and cook for about 5 minutes, or until reduced by half. Whisk in the remaining 4 tablespoons butter, a bit at a time, stirring constantly to prevent separating. Return the crawfish to the sauce and gradually stir in the cream. Lower the heat and cook for about 3 minutes, or until thick and creamy. Season with salt and pepper.

Place equal portions on each of four warm salad plates and garnish with a salted wedge of lime. Serve immediately.

Crawfish Sausage

SERVES 4

1 pound cooked crawfish tail
   meat
½ pound redfish fillet
3 large egg whites
   Salt to taste
   Freshly ground black pepper
   to taste
2 cups heavy cream
2 tablespoons brandy

½ teaspoon cayenne pepper (or
   to taste)
¼ cup finely chopped scallions,
   green part only
½ onion, sliced
1 bay leaf
1 teaspoon black peppercorns
   Cayenne Beurre Blanc (see
   recipe below)

Purée ½ pound of the crawfish meat with the redfish in a food processor fitted with the metal blade. With the machine running, add the egg whites. When the egg whites are thoroughly incorporated, add a generous pinch of salt to firm the mixture (salt coagulates protein, and after the salt is added, there will be a definite change in the texture). Season with black pepper. With the machine still running, gradually add the cream. Transfer the mixture to a bowl and fold in the brandy, cayenne, and scallions, and the remaining ½ pound crawfish. Stir to blend thoroughly.

Fill a deep stock pot with water and add the onion, bay leaf, and peppercorns. Bring the liquid to a boil over high heat. Reduce the heat and let simmer.

To test the sausage seasoning, poach a spoonful of the mixture in the simmering water for 1 minute, then taste. Adjust the seasoning as needed.

Lay approximately 2 feet of plastic wrap on a flat surface. Spoon or pipe a line of the sausage mixture across the wrap, starting 1 inch from either side and 2 inches from the bottom of the wrap. Roll the sausage up tightly in the wrap, tying both ends closed. Place the sausage in the simmering water and poach for 10 minutes, or until firm. Remove from the liquid and drain in a colander.

Carefully unwrap and drain on paper towels. Slice on the bias, into rounds approximately ½ inch thick. Overlap four slices on each of four warm serving plates, and pour the Cayenne Beurre Blanc on top so that it covers half the sausage and pools on the plate. Serve immediately.

The sausage can also be served at room temperature or chilled, with an herbed mayonnaise.

Cayenne Beurre Blanc
MAKES 1½ CUPS

1 shallot, peeled and chopped
1 bay leaf
3 sticks (1½ cups) unsalted butter, softened
1 tablespoon freshly squeezed lemon juice
1 tablespoon white wine vinegar
¼ cup dry white wine
Pinch of freshly ground white pepper
Salt to taste
Cayenne pepper or Windsor Court Pepper (see page 189), to taste

Place the shallot, bay leaf, and 4 tablespoons of the butter in a nonreactive saucepan over medium heat. Sauté for 2 minutes, or until the shallots are translucent. Add the lemon juice, vinegar, wine, and white pepper and cook over medium heat for 5 minutes, or until the liquid is reduced by half. Lower the heat and whisk in the remaining 1¼ cups butter, a bit at a time, being careful not to overheat. When all the butter has been incorporated, strain into a bowl. Season with salt and cayenne pepper or Windsor Court Pepper. Keep warm over warm water until ready to use.

Potted Crawfish

SERVES 4

1 stick (¹/₂ cup) unsalted butter
2 tablespoons ketchup
  Pinch of grated nutmeg
2 tablespoons freshly squeezed
  lemon juice
  Dash of Tabasco sauce

2 tablespoons crawfish fat (if
  available)
  Salt to taste
12 ounces cooked crawfish tail
  meat*

Bring all the ingredients to room temperature.

Cream the butter by hand until it reaches the consistency of mayonnaise. Add the ketchup, nutmeg, lemon juice, Tabasco, and crawfish fat (if available) and blend to form a smooth paste. Season with salt.

Blend the crawfish meat into the butter mixture. Pack into four ¹/₂-cup earthenware pots or ramekins. Chill for about 20 minutes, or until firm. Serve at room temperature in the molds with hot toast points.

* If using frozen crawfish, refresh by boiling the tails for 15 seconds, then plunging them into cold water. Drain well and pat dry.

Oysters Polo

SERVES 6

2 sticks (1 cup) unsalted
  butter, melted
1 cup fresh bread crumbs
3/4 cup grated Parmesan cheese
1 tablespoon herbes de
  Provence
  Salt to taste
  Freshly ground white pepper
  to taste
24 fresh oysters, unshucked
1 small onion, peeled
1 bay leaf

1 whole clove
2 cups milk
6 tablespoons unsalted butter
6 tablespoons all-purpose
  flour
4 tablespoons prepared
  horseradish, drained
  Pinch of grated nutmeg
  Few drops of Tabasco sauce
  (optional)
2½ pounds kosher salt
6 sprigs fresh rosemary

In a bowl, combine the melted butter, bread crumbs, ½ cup
Parmesan cheese, and the herbes de Provence. Stir to blend
and season with salt and pepper. Set aside.

Shuck the oysters, reserving their juice. Discard the flat top
shells. Scrub and dry the bottom shells.

Place the onion, bay leaf, clove, and milk in a small heavy
saucepan over medium heat. When the mixture comes to a
boil, remove the pan from the heat. Reserve and keep warm.

To make the sauce, melt 6 tablespoons butter in a medium

sauté pan over low heat. When the butter is foamy, add the flour and briskly mix together to form a smooth paste. Continue to stir over low heat for 1 minute. Remove from the heat and strain the milk mixture into the paste, stirring constantly. Return the pan to low heat and fold in the remaining ¼ cup Parmesan cheese and the horseradish and nutmeg. Season with salt, pepper, and Tabasco sauce. Cook for 1 additional minute, then turn off the heat.

Fill a large, deep saucepan with water and bring to a boil. Fill a second saucepan or a large bowl with cold water and ice cubes. In the boiling water, poach the oysters for about 1 minute, or just until the edges curl. Remove with a slotted spoon and plunge immediately into the ice water. Drain dry on paper towels.

Preheat the oven to 375 degrees.

Place a layer of rock salt about ½ inch deep in a baker's tray large enough to contain all the oyster shells (use two trays if necessary). Press the empty bottom shells into the salt. Spoon 1 tablespoon of sauce into each shell, then top with an oyster. Cover with another tablespoon of sauce and, finally, a spoonful of buttered herb bread crumbs. Place in the preheated oven and bake for 10 minutes, or until a golden crust forms.

Place four oysters on each of six warm salad plates and garnish with a sprig of fresh rosemary. Serve immediately.

Shrimp Sautéed with Citrus Fruit

SERVES 4

2 oranges, peeled
1 grapefruit, peeled
1 lime, peeled
1 lemon, peeled
1 tablespoon mixed finely
   julienned lime and orange
   zest

2 sticks (1 cup) unsalted
   butter, softened
24 large shrimp, peeled and
   deveined
1/4 cup dry vermouth
   Salt to taste

Over a bowl, segment the fruit, removing all membrane and seeds. Save any juices that collect in the bowl.

Fill a small saucepan with water and bring to a boil. Blanch the julienned zest in the boiling water for 20 seconds. Refresh in cold water. Drain and blot dry. Set aside.

Melt 4 tablespoons of the butter in a heavy skillet over medium heat. Add the shrimp and sauté for 3 to 5 minutes, or until firm and pink. Remove from the pan and wrap in a damp, heated cloth to keep warm and moist. Add the reserved citrus juices and vermouth to the pan. Raise the heat to high and cook for about 3 minutes, or until the liquid is reduced by half. Gently toss the orange, grapefruit, lime, and lemon segments in the reduction. Lower the heat to just below a simmer and cook until the fruit has warmed through.

Remove the pan from the heat and whisk the remaining ¾ cup butter into the mixture, a bit at a time, being careful not to break up the citrus segments. Season with salt. Keep warm.

Place six shrimp on each of four warm serving plates and surround with equal portions of citrus segments. Coat the shrimp with the sauce and garnish with a sprinkling of blanched zest. Serve immediately.

Rillettes of Lobster and Avocado with Cilantro Yogurt Sauce

SERVES 4

1 *two-and-a-half-pound*
  lobster
1 *ripe avocado*
1¹/₂ *teaspoons freshly squeezed*
  lime juice
1 *large egg white*
  Salt to taste
1 *cup heavy cream*

¹/₂ *teaspoon ground cumin*
¹/₂ *teaspoon ground coriander*
¹/₂ *teaspoon Tabasco sauce*
  Freshly ground black pepper
  to taste
  Cilantro Yogurt Sauce (see
  recipe below)

Preheat the oven to 375 degrees.

Fill a large, deep saucepan with water and bring to a boil. With a sharp knife, pierce through the shell and flesh at the cross-shaped mark behind the lobster's head. Blanch in the boiling water for 30 seconds and drain. When cool enough to handle, remove the meat.

Peel the avocado and cut in half. Purée one half in a food processor fitted with the metal blade or in a blender. Evenly slice the remaining half and cover with about ¹/₂ teaspoon lime juice to prevent discoloration. Cover both the purée and the slices with plastic wrap and set aside.

Purée the lobster meat in a food processor fitted with the metal blade or in a blender on medium speed. Add the egg white and ½ teaspoon salt, then gradually incorporate the cream. Add the puréed avocado, cumin, coriander, Tabasco, and remaining teaspoon lime juice and process until well blended. Transfer the mixture to a bowl and adjust the seasoning with salt and pepper.

Divide the mixture equally among four 1-cup ramekins or baking dishes. Fill a baking pan with 2 inches of water. Place the ramekins in this water bath and cover the entire pan with aluminum foil. Bake in the preheated oven for 20 minutes, or until firm to the touch. Remove from the oven. Let cool slightly, then refrigerate for 1 hour, or until well chilled.

Place four salad plates in the freezer to chill.

When the rillettes are well chilled, run a knife around the edge of each ramekin and unmold onto the four chilled plates. Garnish each rillette with avocado slices fanning out to the side of the plate. Serve with Cilantro Yogurt Sauce on the side.

Cilantro Yogurt Sauce

MAKES ½ CUP

¼ cup white wine
2 tablespoons finely chopped fresh cilantro
Pinch of ground coriander
Pinch of ground cumin

1 cup plain yogurt
Dash of Tabasco sauce
Salt to taste
Freshly ground white pepper to taste

Bring the wine to a boil in a small saucepan over high heat. Add the cilantro, coriander, and cumin. Immediately remove from the heat and let cool to room temperature. Fold into the yogurt, add the Tabasco, and season with salt and pepper. If not served immediately, refrigerate, covered, until ready to use.

Crabmeat Soufflé

SERVES 4

4 tablespoons unsalted butter
3 tablespoons grated Parmesan
cheese
3 tablespoons all-purpose flour
4 ounces fresh lump crabmeat,
picked over to remove any
shell and cartilage
1 cup milk, warmed

Pinch of grated nutmeg
Dash of Tabasco sauce
(1/4 teaspoon cayenne pepper
may be substituted)
Salt to taste
Freshly ground white pepper
to taste
5 large eggs

Preheat the oven to 425 degrees.

Using 1 tablespoon butter, generously butter four 1/2-cup soufflé molds. Coat the inside of the molds with 1 tablespoon of the Parmesan cheese.

In a medium saucepan over low heat, combine the remaining 3 tablespoons butter and the flour. Cook for 3 to 4 minutes, or until smooth, then stir in the crabmeat. Slowly pour in the milk, stirring constantly so that the sauce does not become lumpy. Add the remaining 2 tablespoons Parmesan cheese and the nutmeg and Tabasco. Season with salt and pepper. Bring the mixture to a gentle boil, then remove from the heat, transfer to a large bowl, and let cool slightly.

Separate the eggs. Stir the yolks, then fold them into the crabmeat mixture. Set aside.

Whip the egg whites to firm peaks. Fold one quarter of the whites into the crabmeat mixture. Gently fold in the remaining whites, rotating the bowl as they are incorporated. Pour into the prepared molds, being careful not to drip on the sides. Immediately place the filled molds in the preheated oven. Lower the oven temperature to 400 degrees and bake for 30 minutes, or until the soufflés have risen and are golden brown. Do not open the door until the soufflés have baked for 30 minutes. Serve immediately in the molds.

Pâté of Salmon and Crabmeat en Croûte

SERVES 10

2 cups all-purpose flour
1/2 stick (1/4 cup) unsalted butter, chilled
3 tablespoons vegetable shortening, chilled
Salt
1 large egg yolk
5–6 tablespoons ice water
12 ounces salmon fillet, roughly chopped
1/4 cup finely chopped shallots
2 tablespoons finely chopped garlic
1/2 cup finely chopped fresh fennel
1 tablespoon chopped fresh tarragon (1 teaspoon dried tarragon may be substituted)

1/2 cup olive oil
6 ounces fresh lump crabmeat, picked over to remove any shell and cartilage
2 tablespoons diced truffle (optional)
2 tablespoons diced red bell pepper
1/2 cup heavy cream
2 large eggs
Freshly ground white pepper to taste
2 cups dry white wine
2 tablespoons unflavored gelatin
Pinch of saffron

In a large bowl, blend the flour, butter, shortening, and 1½ teaspoons salt with an electric mixer or pastry blender until pea-size crumbs form. Add the egg yolk and as much ice water as necessary just to moisten. Knead into a firm dough. Form into a ball, cover, and refrigerate for at least 1 hour before rolling.

In a second bowl, combine the salmon, shallots, garlic, fennel, and tarragon until thoroughly mixed. Heat the oil in a heavy skillet over high heat until it is almost smoking. Add half the salmon mixture and cook for about 2 minutes, or until just seared. Remove from the pan. Add the remaining salmon mixture and sear as above. Return to the bowl and let cool.

When the salmon has cooled to room temperature, add the crabmeat, truffle, red pepper, cream, and 1 egg. Test the seasoning either by microwaving a tablespoon of the mixture on high for 30 seconds or poaching it for 1 minute in boiling water and tasting. Adjust the seasoning with salt and pepper. Cover and refrigerate.

On a lightly floured surface, roll out two thirds of the dough to a 20- by 14-inch rectangle to line the mold. Roll out the remaining dough into a separate 12- by 6-inch strip that will be used to top the terrine. Let the dough rest for 20 minutes.

Preheat the oven to 350 degrees.

Ease the large rectangle of dough into a 10- by 4- by 4-inch terrine or a 9- by 5 by 2¾-inch loaf pan. Press the dough into the corners of the dish, making sure that 1 inch of dough overlaps the sides.

Fill with the salmon mixture to ½ inch below the top edge of the dish. Smooth the surface, then mound a narrow ridge of salmon, centered, running the entire length of the dish.

Lightly whisk the remaining egg and brush the overlapped edges of dough and the remaining strip of dough with it. Set the top strip, egg-washed side facing down, over the filled dish. Pinch the pieces together all the way around the mold and trim off any excess. About 2 inches from each end of the mold, cut a ¾-inch circle in the top. Brush the top with beaten egg. Place a metal decorating tip or a ball of aluminum foil into each air hole to maintain the opening during baking.

Place in the preheated oven and bake for up to 1 hour, testing after 30 minutes by inserting a metal skewer into one of the breathing holes. If the skewer comes out hot, the pâté is cooked.

Just before removing the pâté from the oven, heat the wine, gelatin, and saffron in a small saucepan over low heat for about 3 minutes, or until the gelatin is completely dissolved.

Remove the pâté from the oven and slowly pour the gelatin mixture alternately through the two breathing holes. When the gelatin begins to seep out of the holes, refrigerate for 15 minutes, then continue to add more gelatin. Refrigerate again, and fill with gelatin until it reaches the top of both holes. If you discover any leaks in the dough, stop adding the gelatin and refrigerate. Plug the leaks with cold butter, then continue to fill with the gelatin. Refrigerate overnight.

Remove any butter plugs and quickly unmold, dipping the terrine in hot water for no more than 5 seconds. Gently tap the pâté away from the sides of the mold and invert onto a platter. Chill for 10 minutes before slicing. Cut into ½-inch slices and place two slices on each of four chilled serving plates.

This pâté may be served with any cold vegetable salad, such as Cucumber Salad (see page 24).

Quenelles of Seafood with Tarragon Cream Sauce

SERVES 4

½ pound firm-fleshed fish
   (salmon, grouper, or
   snapper) or lobster meat
2 large egg whites
   Salt to taste
1¼ cups heavy cream
2 tablespoons brandy
2 tablespoons white wine
   Freshly ground white
   pepper to taste
2 teaspoons chopped fresh
   tarragon

3 cups Fish Stock (see
   page 170)
½ cup dry vermouth
2 tablespoons unsalted butter
2 tablespoons chopped shallots
4 sprigs fresh tarragon
   (optional)
4 teaspoons fresh caviar
   (optional)

Chill all the ingredients thoroughly before beginning the preparation.

Cut the fish or lobster into pieces and purée in a blender or food processor fitted with the metal blade. With the motor running, blend in the egg whites and a pinch of salt. When the mixture begins to stiffen, one item at a time, on a slow speed, gradually incorporate ¾ cup cream, the brandy and wine,

$^1/_8$ teaspoon pepper, and 1 teaspoon chopped tarragon. Transfer to a bowl. Cover and refrigerate for 1 hour.

When the mousse is well chilled, bring the fish stock and vermouth to a simmer in a large, shallow pan over medium heat. Butter a sheet of wax paper. Using two soup spoons dipped in stock, shape spoonfuls of the chilled fish mousse into oval quenelles and place on the wax paper. Drop, one by one, into the barely simmering stock and poach gently, turning once, for 8 to 10 minutes, or until firm. Remove with a slotted spoon and drain on paper towels. Place in a covered dish and keep warm. When all the quenelles have been poached, strain half of the poaching liquid and reserve.

Melt the butter in a medium saucepan over medium heat. Add the shallots and remaining teaspoon chopped tarragon and sauté for about 2 minutes, or until tender. Add the remaining $^1/_2$ cup cream and the strained poaching liquid. Continue to cook until the sauce is thick enough to coat the back of a spoon. Season with salt and pepper.

Arrange four quenelles on each of four warm serving plates and coat with the sauce. Garnish each with a sprig of fresh tarragon or a generous teaspoon of caviar. Serve immediately.

Smoked Redfish with Cucumber Jam

SERVES 4

¹/₂ cup salt
¹/₂ cup sugar
¹/₄ cup minced fresh dill
2 two-pound redfish fillets, skin attached (any deep-water, firm-fleshed fish, such as grouper, cod, or halibut, may be substituted)

1 pound pecan wood chips, soaked in water (any sweet wood chips may be substituted)
Cucumber Jam (see recipe below)
8 thin slices lime

In a small bowl, combine the salt, sugar, and dill. Rub the mixture onto the redfish fillets. Wrap tightly in plastic wrap and refrigerate overnight.

Preheat a smoker according to the manufacturer's instructions. Sprinkle the wood chips over the hot coals. Rinse the redfish under cold running water, pat dry, and place in the smoker. Slowly smoke the fish until firm and flaky, about 8 minutes. Remove from the smoker and refrigerate for about 1 hour, or until chilled. At the same time, place four serving plates in the freezer to chill.

Cut the smoked redfish into ¹/₈-inch-thick slices. Place four slices on each of the chilled plates. Place a spoonful of Cucumber Jam along one side of the fish and garnish with two slices of lime.

Cucumber Jam
MAKES 1 CUP

1 pound European or hothouse cucumbers, peeled, seeded, and sliced (any burpless cucumber may be substituted)
2 tablespoons salt
2 cups sugar

½ cup dry vermouth
1 tablespoon vinegar (malt, cider, champagne, or rice)
1 teaspoon crushed dried red pepper

Sprinkle the cucumber slices with a fine layer of salt and let sit for 20 minutes. Place in a colander and rinse under cold running water. Drain on paper towels. Pat dry. Combine the sugar, vermouth, vinegar, and pepper in a small saucepan over medium-low heat. Bring to a boil. Add the cucumber slices and return the mixture to a boil. Reduce the heat and simmer for 25 to 30 minutes, or until the mixture reaches the consistency of jam. Remove from the heat and let cool. Place in an airtight container and refrigerate until ready to use. Serve cold.

Sautéed Snails with Folsom Chanterelles

SERVES 4

½ stick (¼ cup) unsalted
    butter
24 canned snails, thoroughly
    rinsed and drained
2 tablespoons finely chopped
    shallots
2 cloves garlic, peeled and
    minced
4 ounces Folsom chanterelle
    mushrooms, cleaned and
    sliced (any fresh mushrooms
    may be substituted)

¼ cup white wine
½ cup heavy cream
¼ teaspoon dried thyme
    Salt to taste
    Freshly ground white pepper
    to taste
4 sprigs fresh thyme

Melt the butter in a heavy sauté pan over medium-high heat. Add the snails, shallots, and garlic and sauté for 2 minutes, or until the shallots become translucent. Use a slotted spoon to remove the snail mixture from the pan, allowing any liquid to drain back into the pan. Set the snail mixture aside.

Add the mushrooms to the butter that remains in the pan. Sauté over medium heat for 5 minutes, or until soft. Remove the mushrooms and reserve. With the pan still over medium heat, drain into it any excess juice from the reserved sautéed snails. Stir in the wine, cream, and thyme. Cook, stirring frequently, for 5 minutes, or until reduced by half.

Stir in the reserved snails and mushrooms and cook, stirring frequently, for 3 minutes, or until the mixture is thick enough to coat the back of a spoon. Season with salt and pepper.

Spoon equal portions onto each of four warm serving plates. Garnish with a sprig of fresh thyme and serve immediately.

Fried Frog's Legs with Champagne Mustard Sauce

SERVES 4

1½ cups all-purpose flour
2 large eggs
2 cups beer
   Salt to taste
   Freshly ground white
   pepper to taste
½ stick (¼ cup) unsalted
   butter
2 tablespoons chopped shallots
½ cup Chicken Stock (see
   page 169)

½ cup heavy cream
¼ cup Demi-Glace (see
   page 171)
¼ cup champagne (white wine
   may be substituted)
¼ cup Creole mustard or other
   grainy mustard, or to taste
   Peanut oil for frying
8 pairs small-to-medium frog's
   legs

Sift 1 cup flour into a bowl and make a well in the center. Break the eggs into the well and mix lightly. Slowly add the beer, forming a light batter the consistency of thick cream. Set aside.

Season the remaining ½ cup flour with salt and pepper.

Melt the butter in a sauté pan over medium heat. Add the shallots and cook for 2 minutes, or until translucent. Add the chicken stock, cream, demi-glace, and champagne and cook for about 5 minutes, or until reduced by half. Slowly stir in the mustard. Adjust the seasoning with salt and pepper and remove from the heat. Keep warm.

Heat 1 inch of oil in a heavy skillet until almost smoking. Roll the frog's legs in the seasoned flour, then dip into the beer batter. Place the legs in the hot oil and fry, turning frequently, for about 4 minutes, or until golden brown. Remove from the pan and drain on paper towels.

Coat the bottom of each of four warm serving plates with the mustard sauce. Arrange two pairs of frog's legs on each plate and serve immediately.

Beggar's Purses with Caviar

SERVES 4

½ cup all-purpose flour
1 large egg
¾ cup milk, approximately
1 tablespoon Clarified Butter
   (see page 180)
1 tablespoon snipped fresh
   chives
   Salt to taste
   Freshly ground white pepper
   to taste

2 sticks (1 cup) unsalted
   butter, chilled
¼ cup chopped yellow onion
⅓ cup vodka
2 hard-boiled eggs, peeled and
   finely chopped
2 tablespoons chopped fresh
   parsley
4 ounces Sevruga caviar
4 whole chives, blanched

To make the crêpe batter, sift the flour into a bowl and make a well in the center. Break the egg into the well and whisk to combine the yolk and white. Combine half the milk with the clarified butter and whisk into the flour and egg to form a creamy paste. Continue to add milk until the batter is smooth and thin enough to flow off a spoon in a steady stream. Fold in the chives and a pinch of salt and pepper. Cover and refrigerate for at least 1 hour or overnight.

Remove the crêpe batter from the refrigerator and stir briskly to blend. Lightly grease a small crêpe pan or 6-inch nonstick skillet. Place over medium-high heat and warm until a drop of batter sizzles when it hits the pan. Immediately ladle about 2 tablespoons of batter into the pan, tilting the pan to coat it evenly. Cook, turning once, for about 1 minute, or until golden brown. Remove from the pan and place on wax or parchment paper. Repeat the process until all the batter is used. When the crêpes are completely cool, stack them with wax or parchment paper between them. Four crêpes will be used in the assembly of the Beggar's Purses. You may freeze the remaining crêpes, well wrapped, for future use.

Melt 1 tablespoon of the chilled butter in a sauté pan over medium heat. Add the onion and sauté for 2 minutes, or until translucent. Add the vodka. Raise the heat and bring the mixture to a boil. Let boil for 30 seconds. Remove the pan from the heat and gently whisk the remaining chilled butter into the sauce, a bit at a time. Stir in the hard-boiled eggs and parsley and set aside. Keep warm.

Preheat the broiler.

With the darker sides of the crêpes face down, spoon 2 tablespoons of caviar into the center of each one. Gather up the edge of each crêpe to resemble a drawstring bag and carefully tie with a blanched chive.

Carefully place the tied purses under the broiler for 30 seconds. Immediately place one purse on each of four warm serving plates and surround each purse with an equal amount of sauce. Serve immediately.

Grilled Foie Gras and Pears

SERVES 4

½ cup Poire William or other
  pear-flavored liqueur
1 cup dry white wine
2 ripe pears, peeled, cored, and
  quartered

1 one-and-a-half-pound whole
  duck liver
Salt to taste
Freshly ground black pepper
  to taste

Combine the Poire William and wine in a shallow nonreactive dish. Set aside.

Cut the pear quarters into fans by slicing them, lengthwise, almost but not quite through the stem end. Place the pear fans in the Poire William and white wine and marinate for 1 hour.

Light a charcoal or gas grill.

Pull apart the two lobes of the duck liver. Then, starting from the thin end, cut each lobe diagonally into four ½-inch-thick slices. Season lightly with salt and pepper.

When the grill is red hot, remove the pears from the marinade and lay flat on the hottest part of the grill to score them. Turn and move the pear fans off to the side. Baste with the marinade and grill for 3 to 4 minutes, or until tender.

Place the seasoned liver slices in the center over the hottest part of the grill. Score the liver slices on both sides, then baste with the marinade. Grill for 30 seconds.

Immediately remove the liver from the grill and place two slices at the base of each of four warm serving plates. Arrange two pear fans on each of the four plates above the duck liver slices. Drizzle a little of the marinade on each plate and serve immediately.

Terrine of Chicken and Goose Livers with Cumberland Sauce

SERVES 6 TO 8

6 ounces chicken livers
¹/₄ cup milk
2 ounces pork fat, diced
2 slices bacon, diced
¹/₂ red apple, peeled, cored, and roughly chopped
2 tablespoons chopped shallots
2 tablespoons chopped garlic
¹/₂ teaspoon dried marjoram
¹/₂ teaspoon dried basil
1 teaspoon dried thyme
¹/₄ teaspoon dried rosemary
1 bay leaf
2 tablespoons brandy

2 tablespoons Madeira
2 tablespoons red wine
2 tablespoons sherry
¹/₄ cup peanut oil
¹/₄ cup heavy cream
3 ounces goose liver, diced
¹/₂ ounce black truffle, minced (optional)
Salt to taste
Freshly ground black pepper to taste
Cumberland Sauce (see recipe below)

To cleanse the chicken livers, soak overnight, refrigerated and covered, in the milk. Strain off the milk and dry on paper towels. In a large bowl, combine the chicken livers, pork fat, bacon, apple, shallots, garlic, and herbs. Divide the mixture into four portions and set aside. In another bowl, combine the brandy, Madeira, red wine, and sherry and set aside.

Preheat the oven to 450 degrees.

In a small, heavy skillet, heat 1 tablespoon oil over high heat until smoking hot. Sear one quarter of the liver mixture over high heat, turning once, for about 1 minute, or until the livers are just brown. Transfer to a large bowl. Deglaze the skillet with one quarter of the liquor mixture, then add to the bowl with the cooked livers. Repeat the procedure with the remaining three portions of oil, meat, and liquor. Let cool to room temperature.

Remove the bay leaf and pass the cooled mixture through a meat grinder twice. Fold in the cream, goose liver, and truffle. To test the seasoning, enclose a spoonful of the mixture in a 4-inch square of aluminum foil and cook in a dry skillet placed over high heat for about 30 seconds per side. Taste and adjust the seasoning with salt and pepper, keeping in mind that because the terrine will be served cold, more intense seasoning will be necessary.

Spoon the mixture into a 1-quart loaf pan. Line the bottom of a roasting pan with cardboard for insulation, and place the loaf pan on the cardboard. Fill the roasting pan with 2 inches of hot water. Bake uncovered in the preheated oven for 10 minutes. Reduce the temperature to 300 degrees and cook for an additional 20 minutes.

Press the top of the terrine with a wooden spoon. If the fat surrounding the mixture runs clear, the terrine is done. (Or insert a metal skewer into the middle of the terrine; if the tip comes out hot, the terrine is cooked through.)

Remove the terrine from the oven and let cool to room temperature. Refrigerate, uncovered, for 24 hours. To unmold, dip the loaf pan in boiling water for 10 seconds. Let stand for 30 seconds and invert onto a serving platter. Tap the bottom of the pan and the terrine will slide out.

Cut into ½-inch slices. Serve with slices of unbuttered homemade-type white bread or toast and grapes. Pass the Cumberland Sauce separately.

Cumberland Sauce
MAKES 2½ CUPS

1 cup port wine*
  Grated zest of 1 orange
  Grated zest of 1 lemon
1 cup red currant jelly
  Juice of 1 orange

Juice of 1 lemon
Pinch of cayenne
Pinch of cinnamon
Pinch of ginger

Bring the port wine to a rolling boil in a heavy saucepan over high heat. When boiling, add the orange and lemon zests. Lower the heat and simmer for 20 minutes. Remove the zests with a strainer and reserve. Add the jelly, orange and lemon juices, and seasonings and simmer for an additional 10 minutes. Remove from the heat, add the reserved zests, and let cool to room temperature.

This sauce may be made up to a week in advance. Refrigerate, covered, until ready to use.

* If you are serving game or other more strongly flavored meat, substitute 1 cup Scotch whiskey for the port wine.

Confit of Duck Legs and Lentils

SERVES 4

1 cup dried lentils
2 three-and-a-half- to four-
    pound ducks or 4 whole duck
    legs
1 pound fine kosher salt
½ teaspoon ground allspice
1 bay leaf

2 cloves garlic, peeled
3 cups Chicken Stock (see
    page 169)
1 white or yellow onion, peeled
    and quartered
1 whole clove
1 carrot, peeled

Place the lentils in a large bowl, fill with water to cover, and let
sit overnight.

If using whole ducks, remove the legs. Separate the breasts
from the carcasses, wrap well, and freeze for later use (for
example, in Cashew-Breaded Duck Breasts with Peanut Sauce,
page 115). Reserve the carcasses and trimmings for use in stock.

Place the duck legs in a shallow nonreactive pan and cover
with the salt. Refrigerate for at least 8 hours.

Preheat the oven to 150 degrees.

Rinse the duck legs under cold running water and gently pat
dry. Place in an ovenproof dish, preferably earthenware, and
sprinkle with the allspice. Add the bay leaf and 1 clove garlic.
Pour ½ cup water over the legs, place in the preheated oven,

and roast for 1 hour. Increase the oven temperature to 250 degrees and roast for an additional hour, or until the legs are tender and covered with clear fat.

Drain the lentils thoroughly. Place in a heavy medium-size saucepan and add the chicken stock, onion, remaining clove garlic, whole clove, and carrot. Cover and cook over low heat for about 30 minutes, or until the lentils are tender. Drain off any excess liquid and remove the onion, garlic, clove, and carrot. Keep warm.

Increase the oven temperature to 350 degrees.

Remove the duck legs from the fat and place on a rack in a small roasting pan. Place in the preheated oven and roast for 20 minutes, or until crisp, basting frequently with the fat.

Place an equal portion of lentils and one duck leg on each of four warm serving plates. Serve immediately with slices of warm French bread.

Steak Romanoff

SERVES 4

1 pound beef tenderloin, ground
1 tablespoon finely chopped red
onion
1 tablespoon finely chopped
capers
1 tablespoon finely chopped
parsley
1 teaspoon finely chopped
anchovy, or anchovy paste

Dash of Worcestershire sauce
Dash of Tabasco sauce
Dash of brandy
$^1/_4$ teaspoon freshly ground
black pepper
2 large egg yolks
4 ounces Beluga caviar

Place four salad plates in the freezer to chill.

In a large bowl, combine all the ingredients, except the caviar, with a wooden spoon. Divide into four patties. Place one patty on each of the chilled plates. Cover the top of each patty with 2 tablespoons caviar. Serve immediately with hot buttered toast and chilled vodka.

This recipe can be used for an hors d'oeuvre if presented on toast points served as individual canapés.

IV PASTAS

Pasta Dough

Ziti
with Lobster, Duck, and Cream

Sugarcane Pasta
with Crawfish and Shrimp Stuffing

Shrimp Spaetzle
with Basil Crabmeat Sauce

Pheasant and Juniper Ravioli
with Wild Morel Sauce

Linguine
with Feta, Pancetta, and Baby Artichokes

Pasta Dough

MAKES
APPROXIMATELY
2 POUNDS OF DOUGH

4 cups all-purpose flour
3 large egg yolks
2 large eggs
1 tablespoon olive oil

Pinch of salt
6 tablespoons ice water,
approximately

Sift the flour into a bowl and make a well in the center. Place the egg yolks, whole eggs, oil, and salt in the well and, using a fork or your fingertips, lightly blend the ingredients until evenly moistened. Add the cold water, a little at a time, to form a smooth dough. Turn the dough out onto a lightly floured surface. Gather into a ball. Cover with a damp cloth and refrigerate for at least 30 minutes, or until ready to use.

Using a pasta machine, roll and cut the dough into the desired shape according to the manufacturer's instructions.

Leftover dough can be frozen, well wrapped. When ready to use, defrost, knead lightly, and proceed using a pasta machine, as specified above.

Ziti with Lobster, Duck, and Cream

SERVES 4

1 cup olive oil
8 ounces ziti pasta
4 cloves garlic, peeled and crushed
¼ cup chopped shallots
¼ cup skinned, seeded, and chopped tomato
½ cup white wine
1 tablespoon chopped fresh basil

½ teaspoon crushed dried red pepper
¾ cup heavy cream
½ pound cooked lobster meat, diced
½ pound cooked duck meat, diced
¼ cup grated Parmesan cheese

In a large pot over high heat, bring 3 quarts water and ¼ cup oil to a boil. Add the pasta and cook for 8 minutes, or until al dente. Drain and rinse under warm running water. Drain well and toss with ¼ cup oil. Set aside.

Heat ¼ cup oil in a heavy saucepan over medium-high heat. Add the garlic and shallots and sauté for 2 minutes, or until the shallots are tender. Add the tomato and wine. Sauté for 2 minutes, then add the basil, red pepper, and cream. Continue cooking over medium-high heat for about 5 minutes, or until the liquid is reduced by half.

Preheat the broiler.

Heat the remaining ¼ cup oil in a separate pan over medium-low heat. Add the lobster, duck, and ziti pasta and sauté for 2 minutes, or until heated through. Combine with the cream sauce.

Divide the mixture equally among four ovenproof serving plates. Sprinkle with the Parmesan cheese and place under the preheated broiler for about 30 seconds, or until the cheese has browned. Serve immediately.

Sugarcane Pasta with Crawfish and Shrimp Stuffing

SERVES 6

6 sheets fresh pasta, about 4 by
  6 inches (one half Pasta
  Dough recipe, page 69)
2 ounces peeled raw shrimp
1 large egg white
  Salt to taste
¼ cup heavy cream
  Cayenne pepper to taste
  Freshly ground black pepper
  to taste

2 tablespoons snipped chives
1 tablespoon unsalted butter
2 tablespoons minced shallots
1 tablespoon minced garlic
6 ounces cooked crawfish tail
  meat, chopped
1 large egg, beaten
1 recipe Cayenne Beurre Blanc
  (see page 35)

In a large pot over high heat, bring 2 quarts salted water to a boil. Add the pasta sheets and cook for 3 to 5 minutes, or just until al dente. Drain and reserve between damp cloths.

Purée the shrimp in a blender. Add the egg white and blend thoroughly. Add a pinch of salt and blend. When the mixture begins to stiffen, add the cream, cayenne, and black pepper and blend. Add the chives. Blend on high speed for 30 seconds. Transfer to a bowl. Cover and refrigerate until ready to use.

Melt the butter in a sauté pan over medium-high heat. Add the shallots and garlic and cook for 2 minutes, or until the shallots are tender. Stir in the crawfish tails and remove from the heat. Let cool to room temperature. Fold the crawfish mixture into the shrimp purée and spoon into a pastry bag fitted with a plain tube that has a 1-inch opening.

Line up the pasta sheets, lengthwise, on a flat work surface. Pipe a line of filling down the center of each sheet. Lightly brush the surrounding pasta sheet and the filling with the beaten egg.

With scissors or a sharp knife, make 13 cuts to resemble chevrons about $1/2$ inch apart and at an angle down both sides of the line of filling. Do not cut through the filling. As if making a braid, starting at the top of the right side, fold the first strip over the stuffing, letting it fall across at an angle. Working from the left side, bring the top strip over the right strip. Continue crisscrossing strips, to the bottom of each pasta sheet.

Fill a shallow pan with salted water and bring to a boil.

Ease the stuffed pasta rolls, a few at a time, without crowding, into the boiling water. Cook over medium heat for 3 to 5 minutes, or until the rolls are heated through. Remove from the water with a slotted spoon and drain on a cloth towel. Repeat the process for the remaining pasta rolls. Spoon a portion of Cayenne Beurre Blanc over the surface of each of six serving plates and place a stuffed pasta roll on top. Serve immediately.

Shrimp Spaetzle with Basil Crabmeat Sauce

SERVES 4

8 ounces peeled raw shrimp
2 large egg whites
 Salt to taste
1 tablespoon puréed fresh
 gingerroot
¹/₄ cup puréed shallots
³/₄ cup heavy cream
2 tablespoons sesame oil

Freshly ground white pepper
 to taste
¹/₄ cup Clarified Butter (see
 page 180)
 Basil Crabmeat Sauce (see
 recipe below)
4 large fresh basil leaves

Purée the shrimp in a blender or a food processor fitted with the metal blade. Add the egg whites and blend thoroughly. Add a pinch of salt and run the machine for 30 seconds. The mixture will stiffen considerably with the addition of salt. Add the puréed gingerroot and shallots, cream, and oil and blend. Season with salt and pepper. The mixture should be thick enough to cling to a spoon but should not stick to your fingers. Transfer to a bowl, cover, and refrigerate for 30 minutes.

 In a large pot over high heat, bring 2 quarts of salted water to a rolling boil. Fill a large bowl with ice water. Spoon the shrimp mixture into a spaetzle press.* Holding the press above the pot, push the mixture through the press into the boiling water. Do not overcrowd the pot. Cook for about 1 minute, or until firm. Remove the spaetzle with a slotted spoon and immerse them in the ice water. Drain on paper towels. Repeat the procedure until all the batter is used.

Heat the clarified butter in a large sauté pan over medium-high heat. Add the drained spaetzle and sauté for 3 minutes, or until slightly crisp.

Place equal portions of spaetzle on each of four warm serving plates. Top with Basil Crabmeat Sauce and garnish each plate with a fresh basil leaf. Serve immediately.

Basil Crabmeat Sauce
MAKES 2½ CUPS

1 stick (½ cup) unsalted butter
2 tablespoons minced shallots
1 tablespoon minced garlic
2 tablespoons finely julienned fresh basil leaves, or 1 tablespoon dried
½ cup dry vermouth
½ cup heavy cream

8 ounces fresh lump crabmeat, picked over to remove any shell and cartilage
2 tablespoons finely julienned sun-dried tomatoes
Salt to taste
Freshly ground white pepper to taste

Melt ½ stick butter in a heavy sauté pan over medium heat. Add the shallots, garlic, and basil and sauté for 2 minutes, or until the shallots are tender. Add the vermouth and cream and cook for 5 minutes, or until slightly reduced. Fold in the crabmeat and tomatoes and season with salt and pepper. Stir in the remaining ½ stick butter until well incorporated. Remove from the heat and keep warm until ready to serve.

* If a spaetzle press is not available, put the shrimp mixture in a colander and push it through the holes into the boiling water.

Pheasant and Juniper Ravioli with Wild Morel Sauce

SERVES 4 TO 6

4 cups all-purpose flour
Salt to taste
4 large egg whites
3 tablespoons olive oil
2–4 tablespoons white wine
8 ounces ground pheasant meat (from either the breast or the leg)
1 tablespoon crushed garlic
2 tablespoons minced shallots
1/4 cup gin
1/4 cup heavy cream

Pinch of rubbed sage
Pinch of dried thyme
2 tablespoons grated Parmesan cheese
4 dried juniper berries, crushed
Freshly ground black pepper to taste
1 large egg, beaten
Wild Morel Sauce (see recipe below)
1/4 cup grated Romano cheese

Sift the flour into a bowl with a pinch of salt. Make a well in the center and place the egg whites and 2 tablespoons oil in the well. Using a fork or your fingertips, gradually combine the wet and dry ingredients. Add the wine, a tablespoon at a time, until the mixture pulls together into a firm dough. Form a smooth ball, cover with plastic wrap, and refrigerate for at least 4 hours or overnight.

Combine the ground pheasant with the garlic, shallots, gin, cream, herbs, Parmesan cheese, and juniper berries. When well blended, poach a tablespoon in simmering water for 1 minute and taste to check the seasoning. If necessary, adjust the seasoning with salt and pepper. Set aside.

Using a pasta machine, roll the dough into sheets approximately ⅛ inch thick. Lay half the sheets out on a lightly floured work surface and brush with the beaten egg. Dot each of these sheets with teaspoonfuls of filling spaced 2 inches apart, down the length of the sheets. Cover with the remaining pasta sheets and press gently between the pockets of filling. To cut into individual ravioli, roll a pastry wheel between each mound of covered filling. Make sure the edges are sealed.

Fill a large pot with salted water. Add the remaining tablespoon olive oil and bring to a boil. Add the ravioli, a few at a time, and cook for about 10 minutes, or until al dente. Drain thoroughly.

Place equal portions of ravioli on each of four warm serving plates. Spoon the Wild Morel Sauce over the ravioli and sprinkle with grated Romano cheese. Serve immediately.

Wild Morel Sauce
MAKES 4 CUPS

1 ounce dried morel
   mushrooms, or 3 ounces
   fresh
4 slices raw bacon, finely diced
¼ cup minced shallots
   Pinch of dried thyme
1 clove garlic, peeled and
   crushed

2¼ cups heavy cream
¾ cup Madeira
   Salt to taste
   Freshly ground black pepper
   to taste

If using dried mushrooms, rinse thoroughly and drain. Transfer to a large bowl or pan and rehydrate by covering with boiling water and soaking for 15 to 30 minutes, or until tender. Drain and cut into thin slices. If using fresh morels, simply rinse well and drain, then cut into thin slices.

In a heavy skillet over high heat, bring ½ cup water to a boil. Add the bacon and boil for 2 minutes, to remove most of the salt and grease. Drain and rinse under cold water. Wipe the pan dry. Return the bacon to the pan. Fry over medium heat for 5 minutes, or until crisp. Remove from the skillet and drain on paper towels.

Discard half of the fat from the pan. Add the mushrooms, shallots, thyme, and garlic. Place over medium heat and sauté for 2 minutes, or until the shallots are tender. Add the bacon, cream, and Madeira and simmer for 10 minutes. Season with salt and pepper, being careful not to add too much salt. Keep warm until ready to use.

Linguine with Feta, Pancetta, and Baby Artichokes

SERVES 4

½ pound fresh baby artichokes (bottled artichokes or artichoke hearts may be substituted)
¼ cup olive oil
2 cloves garlic, peeled and crushed
2 ounces pancetta or prosciutto ham, cut into fine strips

¼ pound fresh spinach, stemmed, thoroughly rinsed in salted water, and dried
1 pound linguine, cooked al dente
Salt to taste
Freshly ground black pepper to taste
4 ounces feta cheese, rinsed

Fill a large pot with salted water and bring to a boil.

Remove the small bottom leaves from the artichokes and cut off the stems at the base. Rinse the artichokes and place in the boiling water. Cook for about 10 minutes, or until tender. Rinse under cold running water and cut into quarters. It is not necessary to remove the choke. If using bottled artichokes, drain well, cut into quarters, and set aside until ready to use.

Heat the oil and garlic in a heavy skillet over moderate heat.

Add the pancetta or prosciutto and cook for 1 minute, or until warmed through. Add the quartered artichokes and spinach and cook just until the spinach wilts. Immediately toss with the linguine and season with salt and pepper.

Place equal portions of pasta on four warm serving plates. Crumble the feta cheese over the top and serve immediately.

V FISH AND SHELLFISH

Salmon
with Chinese Mustard Glaze

Rosette of Salmon and Grouper
with Green Peppercorn Sauce

Roasted Salmon
with Watercress Mousse

Red Snapper
with Vanilla

Grilled Grouper
with Frozen Pernod Vinaigrette

Napoleon of Grouper

Tuna
with Two Sesames, Wasabi Beurre Blanc, and Shiitake Mushrooms

Louisiana Crab Cakes
with Fresh Tomato Tartar Sauce

Lobster Poached in Honeyed Water
with Citrus Mayonnaise

Sole Fillets
with Lavender

Grilled Marinated Scallops
with Black Bean Salsa

Harlequin of Three Fish
with Sun-Dried Tomato Sauce

Salmon with Chinese Mustard Glaze

SERVES 4

½ cup dry mustard
½ cup sugar
2 tablespoons clover honey
2 teaspoons soy sauce

Freshly ground black pepper to taste
1 pound mesquite wood chips
4 seven-ounce salmon fillets

In a small bowl, combine the dry mustard and sugar. Add the honey, soy sauce, and 2 tablespoons cold water. Whisk until smooth and thick enough to coat a spoon. If necessary, add more water. Season with pepper and set aside.

Heat some charcoal briquettes in an outdoor grill for 45 minutes, or until white hot. Add the mesquite wood chips and allow to burn for an additional 30 minutes.

Preheat the broiler.

Grill the salmon over the charcoal and mesquite for about 3 minutes on each side (cooking time will depend on the heat of your fire, but do not overcook). Remove the salmon from the grill, carefully peel away any skin, and place the fillets on a broiler pan. Baste with the mustard glaze and place under the broiler for about 1 minute, or until lightly browned.

Place one fillet on each of four warm serving plates. Serve immediately.

Rosette of Salmon and Grouper with Green Peppercorn Sauce

SERVES 4

4 four-ounce salmon strips,
 about ³/₄ inch wide (cut
 lengthwise)
4 four-ounce grouper strips,
 about ³/₄ inch wide (cut
 lengthwise)
¹/₂ cup all-purpose flour
 Salt to taste
 Freshly ground white pepper
 to taste
¹/₄ cup Clarified Butter (see
 page 180) or vegetable oil

2 tablespoons unsalted butter
1 shallot, peeled and finely
 chopped
1 teaspoon green peppercorns,
 crushed
¹/₄ cup brandy
¹/₂ cup heavy cream
¹/₄ cup Demi-Glace (see page
 171) (optional)
¹/₂ cup Beurre Blanc #2 (see
 page 174)

Press one salmon and one grouper strip together and roll up,
forming a rosette. Secure with a wooden toothpick. Repeat the
process with the remaining fish strips. Season the flour with
salt and pepper. Dust the fish rosettes with the seasoned flour.

Heat the clarified butter in a heavy skillet over medium heat.
Add the rosettes and sauté for 3 minutes on each side. Remove
the fish from the pan, drain on paper towels, and keep warm.

Drain the clarified butter from the pan and wipe clean. Add the unsalted butter and melt over medium heat. Add the shallot and peppercorns and sauté for 2 minutes, or until the shallot is soft. Add the brandy and carefully flame. When the flames subside, stir in the cream and demi-glace. Cook for 5 minutes, or until the liquid is reduced by half.

Remove the sauce from the heat and let cool for 2 to 3 minutes. Gradually whisk in the beurre blanc. When well incorporated, season with salt and pepper.

Place one fish rosette on each of four warm serving plates, carefully remove the toothpicks, and spoon the sauce around each rosette. Serve immediately.

Roasted Salmon with Watercress Mousse

SERVES 4

4 six-ounce salmon fillets
Watercress Mousse (see recipe
below)
1 stick (¹/₂ cup) unsalted butter,
melted

Salt to taste
Freshly ground black pepper to
taste

Preheat oven to 375 degrees.

On a flat surface, butterfly the salmon by horizontally slicing almost but not all the way through the fillets. Fold back the newly cut flaps and fill the center of each fillet with Watercress Mousse. Close the flaps and secure with toothpicks.

Brush each stuffed fillet with melted butter and season with salt and pepper. Butter a large roasting pan, place the fillets in the pan, and cover with aluminum foil. Place in the preheated oven and roast for 10 minutes. Remove from the oven. Uncover, carefully peel away any skin, and remove the toothpicks.

Place one fillet on each of four warm serving plates and serve immediately.

Watercress Mousse

MAKES 2 CUPS

1 bunch watercress, stemmed, thoroughly rinsed in salted water, and dried
2 large egg whites, kept separate
4 ounces grouper fillet

Salt to taste
Freshly ground black pepper to taste
1/2 cup heavy cream
Pinch of grated nutmeg

Fill a large pot with salted water and bring to a boil. Blanch the watercress in the boiling water for 30 seconds. Refresh under cold running water, then drain and dry on paper towels.

Whip 1 egg white until blended in a blender or food processor fitted with the metal blade. With the motor running, gradually add the watercress leaves. When the watercress is puréed, transfer to a fine strainer positioned over a bowl. Separately reserve the purée and the liquid that collects in the bowl.

Purée the grouper and the remaining egg white in a food processor fitted with the metal blade. Season with salt and pepper. With the motor running, gradually incorporate the cream. When smooth, add the nutmeg and puréed watercress. Add the watercress liquid, a little at a time, until the mousse is fairly thick and stiff enough to hold its shape. Cover and refrigerate for 15 to 30 minutes, or until ready to use.

Red Snapper with Vanilla

SERVES 4

½ cup all-purpose flour
Salt to taste
Freshly ground white pepper
to taste
4 six-ounce red snapper fillets,
skin attached
¼ cup Clarified Butter (see
page 180)
¼ cup sugar

2 tablespoons champagne
vinegar or white wine
vinegar
1 whole vanilla pod
Grated zest of 2 lemons
¼ cup white wine or vermouth
½ cup Fish Stock (see page 170)
½ cup heavy cream
1½ sticks (¾ cup) unsalted
butter, softened

Season the flour with salt and pepper. Dust the snapper fillets
with the seasoned flour. Heat the clarified butter in a heavy
skillet over medium-high heat. Add the snapper, flesh side
down, and cook, turning once, for 3 minutes on each side, or
until golden brown. Remove the fish from the pan. Drain on
paper towels and keep warm.

Melt the sugar in a small sauté pan over medium heat. When
it begins to turn brown, add the vinegar, vanilla pod, lemon
zest, wine, and fish stock. Raise the heat to medium high and
cook for about 6 minutes, or until reduced by half. Add the

cream and continue cooking until the volume is reduced by a quarter. Lower the heat and gradually whisk in the unsalted butter. Strain, reserving the vanilla pod. Split the pod lengthwise and scrape out the vanilla seeds with the back of a knife. Fold the seeds into the sauce and season with salt and pepper.

Place one snapper fillet on each of four warm serving plates, flesh side up, and spoon the vanilla sauce around each. Serve immediately.

Grilled Grouper with Frozen Pernod Vinaigrette

SERVES 4

1 cup peanut oil
2 tablespoons finely chopped
  shallots
1 tablespoon fennel seeds
¹/₃ cup apple cider vinegar

1 teaspoon freshly ground
  coarse black pepper
1 teaspoon salt
¹/₃ cup Pernod liqueur
4 eight-ounce skinless grouper
  fillets

Heat ¼ cup oil in a skillet over medium-high heat. Add the shallots and fennel seeds and sauté for 2 minutes, or until the shallots are tender. Remove from the heat and let cool slightly. Stir in 2 tablespoons vinegar. When the pan is completely cool, add the pepper and salt, and 2 tablespoons Pernod, and stir to combine. Rub the mixture into the grouper fillets. Cover and refrigerate for 2 hours.

Combine the remaining Pernod, vinegar, and ¾ cup oil in a freezer-proof bowl. Place in the freezer for about 30 minutes, or until slushy, stirring every 10 minutes to prevent separation. The oil in the mixture will never completely freeze.

Prepare a charcoal or gas grill for cooking.

When the grill is hot, sear both sides of the fillets in the center of the grill. Move the grouper to a cooler spot on the grill and continue to cook for about 5 minutes, or until the flesh is flaky and tender. Cooking time will depend upon the thickness of the fish.

Place one grouper fillet on each of four warm serving plates and spoon the frozen vinaigrette over the fish. Serve with Cucumber Salad (see page 24), passed separately.

Napoleon of Grouper

SERVES 4

3 ten- to twelve-ounce grouper
  fillets
Fish Mousse (see recipe below)
Salt to taste
Freshly ground black pepper to
  taste
Watercress Mousse (see
  page 87)

¹/₄ cup vegetable oil
10 romaine lettuce leaves,
  rinsed and dried
 2 cups warm Beurre Blanc #1
  (see page 173)
¹/₄ cup Demi-Glace (see
  page 171)

Preheat the oven to 375 degrees.

Slice the grouper fillets in half lengthwise to make six slices. Pound lightly between wax paper or plastic wrap.

Line a baking sheet with wax paper. Place one piece of grouper on the baking sheet and spread with half of the Fish Mousse. Season lightly with salt and pepper. Cover with a slice of grouper and layer with half of the Watercress Mousse. Season lightly with salt and pepper and top with a piece of grouper. Repeat the process with the remaining ingredients to build a second napoleon.

Brush with the oil and lay the lettuce leaves over the fish

so that they cover the top and sides. Place in the preheated oven and bake for 25 to 30 minutes.

Remove the fish from the oven and let sit for 10 minutes. Slide a spatula under each end and carefully transfer the napoleons to a serving tray. Remove the lettuce leaves and pat the fish dry with a clean cloth. Coat the fish with the beurre blanc. Place the demi-glace in a small pastry bag fitted with a fine tube, and pipe lines on top of the napoleons. Using a toothpick, draw the demi-glace through the beurre blanc to create a marbleized effect.

At tableside, slice the napoleons in half and place a portion on each of four warm serving plates. Serve with Creole Potatoes Dauphine (see page 154) and assorted vegetables.

Fish Mousse
SERVES 4

8 ounces firm fish (salmon, grouper, or snapper) or lobster meat
2 large egg whites
Salt to taste
³/₄ cup heavy cream

2 tablespoons brandy
2 tablespoons white wine
1 teaspoon chopped fresh tarragon
Freshly ground white pepper to taste

Chill all the ingredients thoroughly before beginning the preparation.

Cut the fish or lobster into pieces and purée in a blender or food processor fitted with the metal blade. With the motor running, blend in the egg whites and the salt. When the mixture begins to stiffen, one item at a time, on slow speed so as not to break the mousse, gradually incorporate the remaining ingredients. Adjust the seasoning with salt and pepper. Cover and refrigerate until ready to use.

Tuna with Two Sesames, Wasabi Beurre Blanc, and Shiitake Mushrooms

SERVES 4

4 *eight-ounce tuna steaks*
¼ *cup black sesame seeds*
¼ *cup white sesame seeds*
¼ *cup vegetable oil*
2 *tablespoons sesame oil*
2 *tablespoons wasabi powder (available at Oriental or specialty markets)*
2 *tablespoons heavy cream*

1 *cup Beurre Blanc #1 (see page 173)*
½ *stick (¼ cup) unsalted butter*
4 *ounces shiitake mushrooms, rinsed, dried, and finely sliced (any fresh mushrooms may be substituted)*

Rinse the tuna steaks and pat dry. Combine the black and white sesame seeds on a platter. Press each tuna steak into the seeds, covering both sides well. Heat the oils in a heavy skillet over high heat. Add the tuna and sear for 30 seconds on each side, or until the outside is cooked but still soft to the touch. Remove from the skillet, drain on paper towels, and keep warm.

In a medium bowl, combine the wasabi powder and cream, stirring until the mixture is completely smooth. Add ¼ cup beurre blanc. When well blended, gradually whisk in the remaining ¾ cup beurre blanc. Strain and keep warm.

Melt the butter in a heavy skillet over high heat. When melted, add the mushrooms and quickly sauté for 1 minute, or until soft.

Place one tuna steak on each of four warm serving plates. Top half of each steak with the wasabi beurre blanc and the other half with the sautéed mushrooms. Serve immediately.

Louisiana Crab Cakes with Fresh Tomato Tartar Sauce

SERVES 4 TO 6

6 tablespoons unsalted butter
3/4 cup all-purpose flour
2 cups milk, scalded
  Salt to taste
  Freshly ground black pepper to taste
1 pound fresh lump crabmeat, picked over to remove any shell and cartilage
1/2 medium red bell pepper, stemmed, seeded, and finely chopped
1/2 medium green bell pepper, stemmed, seeded, and finely chopped

1/2 medium yellow bell pepper, stemmed, seeded, and finely chopped
4 scallions (green part only), minced
3 cups bread crumbs, approximately
  Cayenne pepper to taste
1/4 cup Clarified Butter (see page 180) or vegetable oil
  Fresh Tomato Tartar Sauce (see recipe below)

Melt the unsalted butter in a sauté pan over medium heat. Stir in the flour. Lower the heat and cook, stirring, for 3 minutes. Pour in the hot milk, in a steady stream, whisking vigorously until smooth. Season with salt and pepper and simmer over low heat for 10 minutes, stirring often. Remove from the heat and reserve.

In a large bowl, combine the crabmeat, bell peppers, and scallions. Season the bread crumbs with salt, black pepper, and cayenne. Gently mix ½ cup seasoned bread crumbs into the crabmeat mixture. Fold in the reserved white sauce and mix well. Gradually add seasoned bread crumbs until the mixture is not sticky and shapes easily. Form into crab cakes, using about ¼ cup of the mixture for each.

Lightly dredge the crab cakes in the remaining seasoned bread crumbs. Place the clarified butter in a large skillet over medium heat. When the butter is hot, add the crab cakes and fry for 2 minutes on each side, or until golden brown. Drain on paper towels.

Place two crab cakes on each of four warm serving plates, with a dollop of Fresh Tomato Tartar Sauce on the side. Serve immediately.

Fresh Tomato Tartar Sauce
MAKES 3 CUPS

2 fresh tomatoes, peeled, seeded, and finely chopped
2 fresh jalapeño peppers, stemmed, seeded, and finely chopped
12 cornichons, finely chopped
2 tablespoons finely chopped capers
¼ medium onion, peeled and finely chopped
2 cups mayonnaise
Freshly squeezed juice of 2 lemons

Combine all the ingredients in a medium bowl. Cover and refrigerate for 1 hour before serving.

Any leftover sauce may be stored, covered, in the refrigerator for up to 3 months.

Lobster Poached in Honeyed Water with Citrus Mayonnaise

SERVES 4

4 cups honey
2 cups white wine vinegar
2 tablespoons salt
2 oranges, chopped
2 lemons, chopped

2 limes, chopped
1 whole clove
4 one-and-a-half-pound lobsters
    Citrus Mayonnaise (*see recipe
    below*)

Place four serving plates in the freezer to chill.

In a large stock pot over high heat, bring 2 gallons of water to a boil. Add all the ingredients except the lobsters and mayonnaise. Reduce the heat and simmer for 15 minutes. Immerse the lobsters in the water and poach gently for 5 minutes. Remove the pot from the heat and let the lobsters sit in the water for 10 minutes.

Remove the lobsters from the water and split lengthwise by inserting a sharp knife blade where the head joins the body. Remove the tail canals and crack the lobster claws. Remove the top shell from the tails to expose the meat. Lay a lobster tail in its bottom shell on each of the four serving plates, along with the claws. Spoon a generous portion of Citrus Mayonnaise along the center of each lobster tail. Serve immediately.

Citrus Mayonnaise

MAKES 3 CUPS

4 large egg yolks, at room
    temperature
1/2 teaspoon dry mustard
1 tablespoon freshly squeezed
    lime juice
1 tablespoon freshly squeezed
    lemon juice
1 tablespoon freshly squeezed
    orange juice

2 cups walnut oil or vegetable
    oil
Zest of 1 lime, shredded and
    blanched
Zest of 1 lemon, shredded and
    blanched
Zest of 1 orange, shredded
    and blanched

In a blender on high speed, combine the egg yolks, mustard, and citrus juices for 15 seconds. With the motor running, gradually add the oil and blend on medium speed for 1 minute, or until emulsified. Transfer the mayonnaise to a bowl and fold in the zest.

Cover and refrigerate until ready to use. This mayonnaise can be made ahead and stored for 2 or 3 days.

Sole Fillets with Lavender

SERVES 4

4 whole Dover sole, cut into 16 skinless fillets
1/4 cup white wine
1 cup all-purpose flour
Salt to taste
Freshly ground black pepper to taste
1/4 cup Clarified Butter (see page 180) or vegetable oil
1/4 ounce dried lavender blossoms (available at Middle Eastern markets and some specialty food stores)

1 shallot, peeled and minced
1 cup dry vermouth
1 cup Fish Stock (see page 170)
1 cup heavy cream
1/2 stick (1/4 cup) unsalted butter, cut into pieces
4 sprigs lavender

Lay the sole fillets on a flat surface, skin side up, and pound gently to ensure that the fillets do not curl during cooking. Brush with the wine and let sit for 20 minutes.

Season the flour with salt and pepper.

Pat the fillets dry and dust both sides with the seasoned flour. Heat the clarified butter in a heavy skillet over medium heat. Add the fillets and sauté for about 1 minute on each side, or until golden brown. Remove the fish from the pan and drain on paper towels. Keep warm.

Drain the excess butter from the pan. Add the lavender blossoms and shallot and return to low heat. Sauté for 30 seconds, stirring constantly. Add the vermouth and cook for 5 minutes, or until reduced by half. Add the fish stock and continue cooking for about 5 minutes, or until reduced by half. Finally, add the cream and cook for another 5 minutes, or until reduced by half.

Remove the pan from the heat and whisk in the unsalted butter, a bit at a time. Season with salt and pepper. ·

Strain equal portions of sauce onto each of four warm serving plates. Arrange four fillets on each plate and garnish with a sprig of lavender. Serve immediately.

Grilled Marinated Scallops with Black Bean Salsa

SERVES 4

24 large fresh sea scallops
1/2 cup white wine
 1 tablespoon olive oil
   Salt to taste
   Freshly ground black pepper
   to taste

4 strong fresh rosemary
  branches (4 bamboo skewers
  may be substituted)
  Black Bean Salsa (see recipe
  below)

Soak the scallops in cold water for 2 or 3 minutes. Drain, then toss with the wine, oil, salt, and pepper. Cover and refrigerate for 15 minutes.

Prepare a charcoal or gas grill for cooking.

Skewer six scallops on each rosemary branch and cook over the hot fire, turning once, for 2 minutes, or until the scallops are opaque.

Remove from the grill and place one rosemary branch on each of four warm serving plates. Spoon a portion of Black Bean Salsa on the side and serve immediately.

Black Bean Salsa

MAKES 4 CUPS

1 pound dried black beans
Pinch of baking soda
½ yellow bell pepper, stemmed, seeded, and finely chopped
½ green bell pepper, stemmed, seeded, and finely chopped
½ red bell pepper, stemmed, seeded, and finely chopped
1 small red onion, peeled and finely chopped
1 fresh jalapeño pepper, stemmed, seeded, and finely chopped
¼ cup chopped fresh cilantro (or to taste)
½ cup olive oil
2 tablespoons freshly squeezed lime juice
2 tablespoons freshly squeezed lemon juice
1 teaspoon ground cumin
1 teaspoon ground coriander
Salt to taste
Cayenne pepper to taste
Freshly ground black pepper to taste

Pick over the beans, discarding any stones or broken, shriveled, or discolored beans. Place in a large bowl and fill with water to cover. Add a pinch of baking soda and let sit overnight. Drain and place in a large stock pot. Fill with salted water to cover and place over high heat. Bring to a boil, then lower the heat and simmer for about 1 hour, or just until tender. Drain and let cool at room temperature until just warm.

While still warm, combine the beans with the remaining ingredients, seasoning with salt, cayenne, and black pepper. Cover and let sit at room temperature for 2 to 3 hours.

Refrigerate, covered, until ready to use.

Harlequin of Three Fish with Sun-Dried Tomato Sauce

SERVES 4

4 four-ounce tuna strips, ³/₄ by ³/₄ by 4 inches

4 four-ounce grouper strips, ³/₄ by ³/₄ by 4 inches

2 six-ounce skinned salmon fillets

Salt to taste

Freshly ground black pepper to taste

¹/₄ cup all-purpose flour

¹/₄ cup plus 1 tablespoon vegetable oil

10 large outer leaves romaine lettuce, rinsed, dried, and stemmed

Sun-Dried Tomato Sauce (see recipe below)

Lay a strip of tuna and a strip of grouper side by side, lengthwise, on a flat work surface. On top of the grouper strip place a strip of tuna and on top of the tuna strip, place a strip of grouper. Repeat the process until you have formed two stacks of four layers each.

On a flat surface butterfly both pieces of salmon by horizontally slicing almost but not all the way through the fillets so they hinge open. Moisten with water, then place each fillet, hinged open, between two sheets of plastic wrap. Using a meat mallet, lightly pound the fillets into squares large enough to encase the stacked strips. Discard the top pieces of plastic wrap and lightly season the fillets with salt and pepper.

Place one stack of four fish strips in the middle of each salmon square. Grasping the plastic wrap, bring the edges of the salmon up and over the tuna and grouper strips. Lift and roll at the same time so that the tuna and grouper strips are covered with salmon, jellyroll fashion. Peel back and discard the plastic wrap. Secure the salmon with toothpicks.

Preheat the oven to 350 degrees.

Season the flour with salt and pepper.

Lightly dust the salmon packets with the seasoned flour. Heat ¼ cup oil in a skillet over medium heat. Add the salmon packets and sear on all sides. Place the seared salmon on a bed of lettuce and wrap tightly. Brush the leaves lightly with the remaining tablespoon oil. Place the wrapped fish in a shallow ovenproof dish and roast in the preheated oven for 15 minutes.

Remove the salmon from the oven and let sit for 10 minutes, keeping warm. Carefully unwrap the lettuce leaves and discard. Cut each packet horizontally into eight slices. Place four slices on each of four warm serving plates in a diamond configuration. Surround each with Sun-Dried Tomato Sauce and serve immediately.

Sun-Dried Tomato Sauce
MAKES 2 CUPS

½ cup sun-dried tomatoes packed in olive oil (drain olive oil and reserve)

2 shallots, peeled and chopped

1 teaspoon finely chopped fresh basil

1 clove garlic, peeled and crushed

1 bay leaf

1 cup white wine

1 cup heavy cream
  Salt to taste
  Freshly ground black pepper to taste

Finely chop the sun-dried tomatoes, and drain off any remaining oil into a heavy skillet. Add the reserved oil and place over medium heat. When hot, add the tomatoes, shallots, basil, garlic, and bay leaf and sauté until the tomatoes are soft and plump. Stir in the wine and cream and simmer for 10 minutes, or until reduced by half.

Remove from the heat and transfer to a blender. Process at high speed until thoroughly blended. Strain into a clean pan. Place over medium heat and reduce further for 3 to 4 minutes, or until the mixture reaches the consistency of heavy cream. If the sauce seems too thick, thin with a little wine or water. Season with salt and pepper.

Keep warm until ready to serve.

VI FOWL

Chinese Lacquered Duck
with Coffee Mandarin Glaze

Grilled Tea-Marinated Duck Breasts
with Duck Cracklings and Apple Raisin Chutney

J. D.'s Duck Chili

Cashew-Breaded Duck Breasts
with Peanut Sauce

Grilled Chicken Breasts
with Vinegar-Seared Raspberries

Grilled Satay of Chicken
with Ginger Sauce

Cassoulet
with Chicken and White Beans

Stuffed Turkey Breast
with Roast Gravy

Chinese Lacquered Duck with Coffee Mandarin Glaze

SERVES 4

2 four- to five-pound ducks
4 cups coarse salt
2 cups honey
¼ cup sugar
2 tablespoons unsalted butter

½ cup freshly squeezed orange
   juice
½ cup strong black coffee
¼ cup coffee-flavored liqueur
1 teaspoon arrowroot

Rub the ducks thoroughly with the salt and make a small incision in each tail to drain. Place the ducks on a rack set in a shallow pan and refrigerate for 24 hours.

Wash the salt from the ducks under cold running water and remove any excess fat from the skin.

Preheat the oven to 450 degrees.

In a large pot over high heat, bring 2 gallons of water to a boil. Stir in the honey. Immerse the ducks in the boiling honeyed water for 3 minutes. Remove, drain, and set on a wire rack in a roasting pan. Place in the preheated oven and roast for 30 minutes. Reduce the oven temperature to 300 degrees and cook for an additional 45 to 60 minutes, or until the skin resembles black lacquer.

Melt the sugar in a heavy saucepan over medium heat, stirring until it becomes a light brown caramel. Immediately stir in the butter. When the sugar and butter are thoroughly combined, stir in the orange juice, coffee, and liqueur. Simmer for about 3 minutes, or until the sugar dissolves, then stir in the arrowroot to thicken. Remove from the heat and keep warm.

Carve the breasts and legs from the ducks and carefully remove the leg bones, leaving the skin intact. Slice the leg meat and place equal portions on each of four warm serving plates. Slice the breast meat and place above the leg meat on the plate, arranged in a fan pattern. Drizzle with coffee mandarin glaze and serve immediately.

Grilled Tea-Marinated Duck Breasts with Duck Cracklings and Apple Raisin Chutney

SERVES 4

8 teaspoons Lapsang souchong tea leaves (any other smoky-flavored Chinese tea may be substituted)
1/2 cup sugar
1/4 cup salt
4 teaspoons fresh rosemary leaves

1 whole lemon, finely chopped
2 tablespoons honey
8 boneless duck breasts, skin removed and reserved*
Apple Raisin Chutney (see recipe below)

Combine the tea leaves, sugar, 2 tablespoons salt, rosemary, lemon, and honey in a large glass bowl. Pour 4 cups boiling water over the mixture. Let cool to room temperature.

Place the skinned duck breasts in the tea marinade, cover, and refrigerate for 8 hours.

Cut the reserved duck skin into strips approximately 1/4 inch

* If boned duck breasts are unavailable, purchase four whole ducks. Debone and freeze the leg meat for another use, such as in J. D.'s Duck Chili (page 113).

wide. Combine the strips with the remaining 2 tablespoons salt and let sit at room temperature for 2 hours. Rinse thoroughly under cold running water to remove the salt and pat dry.

Combine the strips of skin with ¼ cup water in a skillet over high heat. Cook until the water has evaporated and the strips have become brown and crispy in the rendered fat. Drain on paper towels and keep warm.

Prepare a charcoal or gas grill for cooking.

Remove the duck breasts from the marinade, and wipe dry. Place on the hot grill and cook, turning once, for approximately 4 minutes on each side, or until medium rare.

Place two duck breasts on each of four warm serving plates. Spoon a portion of Apple Raisin Chutney alongside and sprinkle the cracklings on top. Serve immediately.

Apple Raisin Chutney
MAKES 4 CUPS

³/₄ pound Granny Smith apples, peeled, cored, and finely chopped
1 cup packed light brown sugar
½ cup apple cider vinegar
1 teaspoon salt
½ teaspoon ground ginger
¼ green bell pepper, seeded and chopped
¼ medium yellow onion, peeled and finely chopped
½ cup golden raisins
Juice and grated zest from ½ lemon

Combine the apples, brown sugar, vinegar, salt, and ginger in a saucepan over medium heat. Bring to a boil, stirring frequently. Lower the heat and simmer for 10 minutes. Add the green pepper, onion, raisins, lemon juice, and lemon zest and return to a boil. Stirring frequently, simmer for 1 hour, or until thickened.

Remove from the heat and keep warm.

Apple Raisin Chutney may be made ahead and stored, covered, in the refrigerator until ready to use. Reheat before serving.

J. D.'s Duck Chili

SERVES 6 TO 8

1 four-and-a-half- to five-pound duck
1 teaspoon cayenne pepper
1 tablespoon paprika
1 tablespoon chili powder
1 teaspoon ground cumin
1 teaspoon ground coriander
1 cup dried kidney beans
2 cups finely chopped onion
1 carrot, peeled and finely chopped
2 stalks celery, trimmed and finely chopped
9 cloves garlic, peeled, 3 kept whole, 6 finely chopped
6 bay leaves
2 tablespoons chopped fresh thyme
1 tablespoon chopped fresh rosemary

1 tablespoon black peppercorns
6 slices raw bacon, chopped
1/4 cup seeded and finely chopped fresh jalapeño pepper (or to taste)
1/2 cup finely chopped red bell pepper
1/2 cup finely chopped green bell pepper
2 very ripe tomatoes, peeled and chopped (1 sixteen-ounce can whole tomatoes may be substituted)
6 ounces tomato paste
1 tablespoon chopped fresh cilantro
Salt to taste
Freshly ground black pepper to taste

Debone the duck and dice the meat. Reserve the bones; discard the fat and skin. In a small bowl, combine the cayenne pepper, paprika, chili powder, cumin, and coriander. Generously coat the duck with the spices, then cover with plastic wrap and refrigerate for 8 hours.

Pick over the beans, discarding any stones or broken, shriveled, or discolored beans. Place in a large bowl, fill with water to cover, and let sit for at least 8 hours.

Place 1½ quarts of water in a large pot. Add the duck bones and place over high heat. Bring to a simmer and cook for 15 minutes, skimming any scum that forms on the surface. Add 1 cup onion, the carrot and celery, the whole garlic cloves, 4 bay leaves, 1 tablespoon thyme, the rosemary, and the black peppercorns. Simmer, uncovered, for 2 to 3 hours. Strain. (This may be done a day in advance and stored, covered, in the refrigerator. Skim off the fat from the top of the cold stock before using.)

Combine the bacon with ½ cup water in a large heavy pot over medium heat. Cook until the water has evaporated and the bacon has become crispy in the rendered fat. Remove the bacon with a slotted spoon and reserve. Increase the heat until the fat remaining in the pan is almost smoking hot. Add the duck meat and quickly sear all sides. Add the remaining onion, along with the chopped garlic, jalapeño, and bell peppers. Lower the heat to medium and sauté for 2 minutes, or until the onion is tender. Stir in the tomatoes and tomato paste. Reduce the heat to low and cook for 5 minutes.

Drain the beans. Add to the chili, along with the bacon, stock, remaining tablespoon thyme and 2 bay leaves, and cilantro. Let simmer for 1½ hours. Adjust the seasoning with salt and pepper.

Serve hot in warm serving bowls.

Cashew-Breaded Duck Breasts with Peanut Sauce

SERVES 4

4 six-ounce skinless, boneless
   duck breasts
2 tablespoons salt
³/₄ cup finely ground unsalted
   cashew nuts
¹/₂ cup bread crumbs
   All-purpose flour

Salt to taste
Freshly ground black pepper
to taste
Egg Wash (see page 190)
¹/₄ cup Clarified Butter (see
   page 180) or vegetable oil
   Peanut Sauce (see recipe below)

Rub the duck breasts with the salt and let sit for 2 hours at room temperature. Rinse thoroughly under cold running water to remove salt and pat dry.

Combine the ground cashews and bread crumbs in a shallow dish. Season the flour with salt and pepper. Dust the duck breasts with the seasoned flour. Dip in the egg wash, then coat with the bread crumb mixture.

Heat the butter in a heavy skillet over medium-high heat. Add the duck breasts and sauté, turning once, for about 4 minutes, or until medium rare and browned on both sides.

Place the duck breasts on four warm serving plates. Serve immediately with a pool of Peanut Sauce on the side.

Peanut Sauce

MAKES 2 CUPS

2 fresh jalapeño peppers,
  stemmed and seeded
2 cloves garlic, peeled
1 tablespoon peanut oil
1/2 cup canned unsweetened
  coconut milk*
1 tablespoon soy sauce
2 tablespoons Oriental fish
  sauce (available at Oriental
  groceries and some
  supermarkets)

1 1/2 teaspoons rice wine vinegar
1 tablespoon honey
1 tablespoon chopped fresh
  cilantro
1 cup creamy peanut butter

Combine the jalapeños, garlic, and oil in a blender or food processor fitted with the metal blade and process for 30 seconds. Add the coconut milk, soy sauce, fish sauce, vinegar, honey, and cilantro and process for an additional 30 seconds. Add the peanut butter and pulse the machine until the ingredients are well blended and the sauce is smooth. Serve at room temperature.

Peanut sauce can be made ahead and stored, covered, in the refrigerator for up to 3 months.

* If canned coconut milk is unavailable, you can make your own by steeping 3/4 cup unsweetened shredded coconut in 3/4 cup milk for 30 minutes over low heat. Strain, forcing as much of the milk as possible out of the coconut.

Grilled Chicken Breasts with Vinegar-Seared Raspberries

SERVES 4

2 teaspoons vegetable oil
2 cloves garlic, peeled and minced
2 teaspoons minced dried lemon peel
2 teaspoons honey
Salt to taste
Freshly ground black pepper to taste

4 whole skinless, boneless chicken breasts
1/4 cup raspberry vinegar
1 pint raspberries, rinsed and dried
2 tablespoons brown sugar

In a small bowl, combine the oil, garlic, lemon peel, honey, salt, and pepper to make a paste. Gently rub into both sides of the chicken breasts.

Prepare a charcoal grill for cooking, preferably with mesquite wood.

Place the chicken breasts over a hot fire and cook for 4 to 5 minutes on each side, or until the flesh is firm and white. Transfer to a covered dish and keep warm.

Heat a small skillet over high heat until very hot. Add the

vinegar, which will boil instantly, and the raspberries. Remove from the heat and stir in the brown sugar.

Place one chicken breast on each of four warm serving plates. Coat with the hot raspberry sauce and serve immediately.

Grilled Satay of Chicken with Ginger Sauce

SERVES 4

4 six-ounce skinless, boneless chicken breasts
2 large egg whites, lightly beaten

2 tablespoons soy sauce
2 tablespoons honey
Ginger Sauce (see recipe below)

Cut the chicken breasts into strips 2 inches by ½ inch. Place in a shallow dish, coat with the egg whites, and let sit for 1 hour at room temperature.

Prepare a charcoal or gas grill for cooking, or preheat a griddle on the stove over high heat.

Combine the soy sauce and honey in a medium bowl. Remove the chicken from the egg whites, rinse, and pat dry. Toss the chicken strips in the soy-honey mixture and thread onto four wooden skewers. Place on the hot grill or griddle and cook, turning occasionally, for 10 to 15 minutes, or until golden brown.

Place one skewer on each of four warm serving plates. Drizzle Ginger Sauce over the chicken and serve immediately.

Ginger Sauce

MAKES 1 CUP

½ cup sugar
1 tablespoon unsalted butter
2 tablespoons chopped fresh
  gingerroot
2 tablespoons freshly squeezed
  lemon juice
Pinch of cayenne pepper

2 tablespoons honey
¼ cup Chicken Stock (see page
  169)
Salt to taste
Freshly ground white pepper
to taste

In a heavy saucepan over medium heat, dissolve the sugar in 2 tablespoons water. Stirring frequently, cook for about 5 minutes, or until the mixture begins to turn brown. Do not allow to burn. Stir in the butter, ginger, lemon juice, cayenne, honey, and chicken stock. Reduce the heat to low and simmer for 2 to 3 minutes, or until the sauce thickens slightly. Strain and season with salt and pepper. Keep warm until ready to serve.

Cassoulet with Chicken and White Beans

SERVES 6 TO 8

1 pound dried navy beans
1/2 pound raw bacon
1 onion, peeled and diced
4 cloves garlic, peeled and
   minced
1/4 teaspoon fresh thyme
   Pinch of ground clove
4 cups Chicken Stock (see
   page 169)

1/2 teaspoon salt
   Pinch of freshly ground black
   pepper
4 ounces andouille or other
   hot, spicy sausage
2 whole smoked boneless
   chicken breasts
1/4 cup bread crumbs

Pick over the beans, discarding any stones or beans that are broken, shriveled, or discolored. Place in a large bowl, fill with cold water to cover, and let sit for 3 hours.

Dice half the bacon and place in a skillet over medium heat. Fry for 5 minutes, or until crisp. Remove from the pan, drain on paper towels, and reserve. Strain the bacon grease from the skillet into a large pot. Add the onion, garlic, thyme, and clove to the pot. Place over medium heat and sauté for 2 minutes, or until the onion becomes translucent.

Drain the beans and add, along with the chicken stock, to

the pot. Bring the mixture to a boil over high heat. Lower the heat and season with salt and pepper. Let simmer for 2 hours, or until the beans are soft but have not begun to break apart and the liquid has reduced by half.

Slice the sausage into ¼-inch-thick rounds. Place in a heavy skillet over medium heat. Stirring frequently, sauté for 5 minutes, or until well browned.

Cut the chicken into bite-size pieces.

Preheat the oven to 325 degrees.

Spoon half the cooked beans into a large ovenproof casserole. Layer with chicken, then cooked bacon, then sausage, and finally the remaining beans. Slice the remaining raw bacon and scatter over the beans. Sprinkle with the bread crumbs. Place in the preheated oven and bake for 1½ hours.

Serve hot in warm serving bowls.

Stuffed Turkey Breast with Roast Gravy

SERVES 4 TO 6

1 three- to four-pound boneless turkey breast, skin attached
Salt to taste
Freshly ground black pepper to taste
¼ cup white truffle-flavored olive oil (*plain olive oil may be substituted*)
4 ounces prosciutto ham, finely shredded
¼ cup finely chopped shallots

4 cloves garlic, peeled and minced
2 teaspoons ground sage
½ cup bread crumbs
2 cups Chicken Stock (*see page 169*)
⅓ cup grated Parmesan cheese
⅓ cup grated Romano cheese
½ cup white wine
½ cup Marsala

Place the turkey breast, skin side down, on a cutting board. Butterfly the breast by slicing horizontally almost but not all the way through the meat, leaving about a ½-inch hinge at the opposite edge. Lay the breast on a large sheet of aluminum foil with the flap open. Season with salt and pepper.

Heat the oil in a heavy skillet over medium-high heat. Add the prosciutto, shallots, garlic, and sage and sauté for 2 minutes, or until the shallots are tender. Remove from the heat and let cool. Fold in the bread crumbs, 1 cup chicken stock, and the grated cheeses. Mix well and adjust the seasoning with salt and pepper.

Preheat the oven to 375 degrees.

Place the stuffing in the center of the turkey breast. Fold the flap over the stuffing. Wrap the breast with the foil and place in a roasting pan. Place in the preheated oven and bake for 1 hour. If desired, fold back the foil and brown the top of the breast during the last 10 to 15 minutes of roasting.

Remove the turkey from the oven and let sit on a platter for 10 minutes, still covered with the foil.

Place the roasting pan over high heat and deglaze with the white wine, Marsala, and remaining cup chicken stock, scraping any brown bits from the bottom of the pan with a wooden spoon. Lower the heat to medium and cook for 4 minutes, or until slightly reduced. Adjust the seasoning with salt and pepper and strain into a small pan. Unwrap the turkey and drain any juice into the gravy. Skim the grease from the surface and transfer the gravy to a sauce boat.

Slice the breast and place on a serving platter. Serve warm with the gravy on the side.

VII GAME

Roasted Abita Springs Quail
with Port-Coriander Sauce

Panéed Loin of Rabbit Thermidor

Wild Fowl Braised with Port

Medallions of Venison
with Chanterelles

Roasted Abita Springs Quail with Port-Coriander Sauce

SERVES 4

1 cup bread crumbs
2 tablespoons herbes de
   Provence
   Pinch of cayenne pepper
8 boneless Abita Springs
   quail (other quail may be
   substituted)
¹/₄ cup Creole mustard or other
   grainy mustard
¹/₄ cup all-purpose flour
1 cup Egg Wash (see
   page 190)
³/₄ cup vegetable oil
¹/₄ cup Clarified Butter (see
   page 180) or vegetable oil

2 shallots, peeled and finely
   chopped
1 teaspoon ground coriander
1 cup Demi-Glace (see
   page 171)
¹/₂ cup port wine
¹/₄ cup honey
¹/₂ stick (¹/₄ cup) unsalted
   butter
   Salt to taste
   Freshly ground black pepper
   to taste
1 bunch watercress, stemmed,
   thoroughly rinsed in salted
   water, and dried

On a plate, combine the bread crumbs, herbes de Provence, and cayenne. Coat the quail with the mustard, then dust with the flour. Dip in the egg wash, then press into the seasoned bread crumbs.

Heat the oil in a heavy skillet over high heat. Add the quail and sauté, turning once, for 5 minutes, or until golden brown. Remove from the pan, drain on paper towels, and keep warm.

Heat the clarified butter in a saucepan over medium heat. Add the shallots and coriander and sauté for 2 minutes, or until the shallots are soft, then add the demi-glace, port, and honey. Bring to a low boil and cook for about 5 minutes, or until thick enough to coat the back of a wooden spoon. Remove from the heat and whisk in the butter, a piece at a time. Season with salt and pepper.

Spoon equal portions of sauce onto each of four warm serving plates and arrange two quail on each plate. Garnish with the watercress leaves and serve immediately.

Panéed Loin of Rabbit Thermidor

SERVES 4

3/4 cup bread crumbs
2 tablespoons herbes de Provence
1 cup all-purpose flour
Salt to taste
Freshly ground white pepper to taste
8 rabbit loins, trimmed of fat and silverskin
1 cup Egg Wash (see page 190)

1/4 cup Clarified Butter (see page 180) or vegetable oil
2 tablespoons dry mustard
3/4 cup Béchamel Sauce (see page 175)
2 tablespoons grated Parmesan cheese
4 large egg yolks
1/4 cup heavy cream

On a plate, combine the bread crumbs and herbes de Provence. Season the flour with salt and pepper. Dust the rabbit loins with the seasoned flour, dip in the egg wash, then roll in the seasoned bread crumbs.

Heat the clarified butter in a heavy skillet over high heat. Add the breaded rabbit. Lower the heat to medium and sauté, turning frequently, for about 2 minutes, or until lightly browned. Remove from the pan and drain on paper towels. Keep warm.

Preheat the broiler.

In a medium bowl, combine the mustard and a little water to make a smooth paste. Whisk in the béchamel, Parmesan, and egg yolks. Whip the cream to hold firm peaks, then fold gently into the mustard mixture.

Coat the bottom of four ovenproof dinner plates with the mixture. Place under the preheated broiler and broil for 30 seconds, or until golden brown. Broil only one plate at a time and watch carefully to prevent scorching.

Slice the rabbit and arrange two loins on each sauce-glazed plate. Serve immediately.

Omelette Linley (PAGE 197)

Red Snapper with Vanilla (PAGE 88)

Roasted Abita Springs Quail with Port-Coriander Sauce (PAGE 127)

Vegetable Terrine, Chanterelle and Tomato Soup, Harlequin of Three Fish with Sun-Dried Tomato Sauce, and Sorbets with Plumes

Chanterelle and Tomato Soup
(PAGE 11)

Vegetable Terrine (PAGE 157)

*Harlequin of Three Fish
with Sun-Dried Tomato Sauce*
(PAGE 104)

Napoleon of Grouper (PAGE 92)

Grilled Veal Chops with Billy's Mother's Caponata Relish (PAGE 143)

Grilled Foie Gras and Pears (PAGE 59)

Steak Romanoff (PAGE 66)

Harlequin Mask with Trio of Sorbets (PAGE 241)

Chocolate Breathless (PAGE 224)

Smoked Redfish (PAGE 51)

Chinese Lacquered Duck with Coffee Mandarin Glaze (PAGE 109)

Lobster Poached in Honeyed Water with Citrus Mayonnaise (PAGE 98)

Sugarcane Pasta with Crawfish and Shrimp Stuffing (PAGE 72)
Baby Lettuces with Lemon Parmesan Vinaigrette (PAGE 20)

Tuna with Two Sesames, Wasabi Beurre Blanc, and
Shiitake Mushrooms (PAGE 94)

Hot Crawfish with Gingered Sesame on Watercress (PAGE 25)

Louisiana Crab Cakes (PAGE 96)

Oysters Polo (PAGE 38)

Wild Fowl Braised with Port

SERVES 4

1 bottle port wine
½ cup red wine vinegar
  Sprig of fresh thyme
  Sprig of fresh rosemary
4 bay leaves
10 dried juniper berries,
  crushed
4 cloves garlic, peeled and
  crushed
6 black peppercorns, crushed
1 large onion, peeled and
  chopped

4 whole wild ducks (teal,
  mallard, or widgeon) or
  geese
½ cup vegetable oil
¼ cup tomato paste
4 cups Chicken Stock (see
  page 169)
6 slices whole wheat bread,
  torn into pieces
1 cup Burgundy wine
1 teaspoon grated unsweetened
  dark chocolate (optional)

In a large nonreactive bowl deep enough to hold the ducks or geese, combine the port, vinegar, thyme, rosemary, bay leaves, juniper berries, garlic, peppercorns, and onion. Add the birds and let sit for 1 week in the refrigerator, turning every day.

Drain the birds. Strain the marinade, reserving the liquid and solids separately.

Preheat the oven to 350 degrees.

Heat the oil over high heat in a heavy skillet or roasting pan large enough to accommodate all four birds at once. Add the birds and quickly sear on all sides. Remove the birds and add the reserved solids from the marinade to the pan. Lower the heat to medium and cook for 2 minutes, or until the onion is translucent. Add the tomato paste and cook, stirring constantly, for 3 minutes, or until the mixture turns a rich brown. Stir in the chicken stock and bread, then add the Burgundy and half of the reserved liquid from the marinade.

When the mixture comes to a boil, return the birds to the pan, breast side down. Cover and place in the preheated oven. Braise for about 1½ hours, or until the breasts are tender. The exact cooking time will depend on the texture of the birds.

Remove the birds from the pan and keep warm. Strain the cooking liquid into a clean saucepan. Place over low heat and cook until the liquid has reduced to the desired taste; the longer the liquid is cooked, the stronger the game flavor. If an even stronger game flavor is desired, add the remaining liquid from the marinade and continue reducing. If a smoother sauce is desired, add the grated chocolate, but do not let the sauce boil after this addition. Strain and reserve, keeping warm.

Carve the legs from the ducks and carefully remove the leg bones, leaving the skin intact. Slice the leg meat and place equal portions on each of four warm serving plates. Slice down both sides of each breast and peel the breast meat away. Arrange on top of the leg meat. Spoon the sauce over the meat and serve immediately, with fall vegetables such as baked potatoes, carrots, turnips, or glazed onions.

Medallions of Venison with Chanterelles

SERVES 4

1/4 cup Clarified Butter (see page 180) or vegetable oil
8 three-ounce medallions of venison, cut from the loin or tenderloin
6 ounces chanterelle mushrooms, rinsed, dried, stemmed, and sliced (any fresh mushrooms may be substituted)

1 clove garlic, peeled
2 shallots, peeled and chopped
1 bay leaf
1/4 cup Madeira
1/2 cup heavy cream
1/4 cup Demi-Glace (see page 171)
Salt to taste
Freshly ground black pepper to taste

Heat the clarified butter in a heavy skillet over high heat. Add the venison medallions and sauté, turning once, for about 2 minutes, or until medium rare. Remove from the pan and set aside. Keep warm.

Drain half the butter from the pan. Return the pan to medium-high heat and add the mushrooms, garlic, shallots, and bay leaf. Sauté for 2 minutes, or until the shallots are soft. Remove the mixture from the pan with a slotted spoon and discard the garlic clove and bay leaf. Transfer the shallots and mushrooms to a covered dish and keep warm.

Drain any remaining butter from the pan. Return the pan to high heat and add the Madeira, stirring constantly to deglaze the pan. Stir in the cream and demi-glace. Lower the heat and simmer for about 5 minutes, or until the sauce is slightly reduced.

Remove from the heat and stir in the mushrooms and shallots. Season with salt and pepper and add any juice drained from the medallions.

Place two venison medallions on each of four warm serving plates. Coat one medallion with the sauce and leave the other uncovered. Serve immediately. Pass extra sauce separately.

VIII MEATS

Lamb Chops
with Indian Spinach Sauce

Grilled Rack of Lamb
with Cumin Coriander Bordelaise

Chiffonade of Lamb
with Basil Pesto

Grilled Veal Chops
with Billy's Mother's Caponata Relish

Roulade of Veal
with Spinach, Pine Nuts, and Crabmeat, and Marsala Sauce

Roast Tenderloin of Beef
with Creole Cardinal Sauce

Tournedos of Beef
with Red Butter and Beef Marrow

Lamb Chops with Indian Spinach Sauce

SERVES 4

¹/₄ cup Clarified Butter (see
page 180) or vegetable oil
12 French-trimmed lamb chops
(trim away as much excess
fat as possible)
1 yellow onion, peeled and
finely chopped
4 cloves garlic, peeled and
minced
1 teaspoon minced fresh
gingerroot

¹/₂ cinnamon stick
1 teaspoon ground coriander
Pinch of turmeric
Pinch of cayenne pepper
2 whole cardamom seeds or ¹/₄
teaspoon ground cardamom
1 cup cooked chopped spinach
¹/₄ cup heavy cream
Salt to taste
Freshly ground black pepper
to taste

Heat the butter in a heavy skillet over medium-high heat. Add the lamb chops and sauté, turning once, for about 6 minutes, or until medium rare. Remove from the pan, drain on paper towels, and keep warm.

Pour off all but 2 tablespoons fat from the pan. Return the pan to medium heat. Add the onion, garlic, and ginger and sauté for 2 minutes, or until the onion is translucent. Add the cinnamon, coriander, turmeric, cayenne, and cardamom. Lower the heat and cook for 1 minute. Stir in the chopped spinach and cream and simmer for 3 to 4 minutes. Remove the cinnamon stick from the pan and season with salt and pepper.

Spoon equal portions of spinach sauce onto each of four warm serving plates. Place three chops on each bed of spinach and serve immediately.

Grilled Rack of Lamb with Cumin Coriander Bordelaise

SERVES 4

2 racks of lamb
2 tablespoons ground coriander
2 tablespoons ground cumin
1 tablespoon garlic powder
1 teaspoon dried rosemary
1/2 teaspoon salt
1/3 cup freshly squeezed lime
   juice

1/4 cup olive oil
1 teaspoon Worcestershire
   sauce
1 tablespoon vegetable oil
   Cumin Coriander Bordelaise
   (see recipe below)

Using a cleaver, cut the chine bone (backbone) from the racks. Trim away the fat and sinew from under the ribs. Cut out the meat between the bones and scrape the bones clean on all sides.*

In a small bowl, combine the coriander, cumin, garlic, rosemary, and salt. Stir in the lime juice, olive oil, and Worcestershire to form a smooth paste. Rub the mixture into the lamb racks and let sit for 4 hours at room temperature.

Preheat the oven to 375 degrees.

* If you prefer, ask your butcher to French-trim the racks of lamb for you.

Place the vegetable oil in a large heavy skillet and heat almost to smoking. Add the racks and sear until brown on all sides.

Place the browned lamb in a large roasting pan in the preheated oven and roast for 15 minutes for medium rare (or longer, according to your preference).

Remove from the oven and let sit for 5 minutes. Slice each rack into four thick chops, with two bones in each chop. Place two chops on each of four warm serving plates and spoon a portion of Cumin Coriander Bordelaise alongside. Serve immediately.

Cumin Coriander Bordelaise

MAKES 1½ CUPS

2 tablespoons Clarified Butter (*see page 180*) *or vegetable oil*
2 shallots, peeled and finely chopped
½ teaspoon ground cumin
½ teaspoon ground coriander
1 tablespoon freshly squeezed lime juice

¼ cup dry vermouth
1 cup Demi-Glace (*see page 171*)
Salt to taste
Freshly ground black pepper to taste

Heat the butter in a small saucepan over medium heat. Add the shallots, cumin, and coriander and sauté for 3 minutes, or until the shallots are tender. Add the lime juice, vermouth, and demi-glace and simmer for 5 minutes. Season with salt and pepper. Strain and keep warm until ready to serve.

Chiffonade of Lamb with Basil Pesto

SERVES 4

1 *two-and-three-quarter-pound leg of lamb, trimmed of fat and sinew*
¼ *cup olive oil*

2 *tablespoons freshly ground black pepper*
½ *cup Basil Pesto (see recipe below)*

Cut the lamb into strips ¼ inch wide by 2 inches long. Toss with the oil and black pepper in a shallow dish. Cover and refrigerate for 8 hours.

Heat a 10-inch cast-iron skillet over high heat until extremely hot. Place the lamb in the skillet in a single layer and press down with a flat lid or plate to sear. Flip the lamb onto the lid or plate, slide the meat carefully back into the skillet, and press down to sear the other side. Brush ¼ cup Basil Pesto over the lamb and remove from the heat. Place a serving platter on top of the skillet and quickly invert so that the lamb will fall onto the platter in one piece. Brush the top side of the lamb with the remaining ¼ cup Basil Pesto. (If the lamb does not fit into the skillet in a single layer, divide the meat and Basil Pesto in half and cook in two stages.)

Divide the lamb into four wedges and transfer to four warm

serving plates. Serve immediately with Linguine with Feta, Pancetta, and Baby Artichokes (see page 79) or Cilantro and Turmeric Pilaf (see page 163).

Basil Pesto
MAKES 3 CUPS

10 cloves garlic, peeled
1½ cups fresh basil leaves,
    rinsed and dried
⅔ cup toasted pine nuts
½ cup grated Parmesan cheese
½ cup grated Pecorino or
    Romano cheese

1–1¼ cups olive oil
    Salt to taste
    Freshly ground black
    pepper to taste

Combine the garlic, basil, pine nuts, and grated cheeses with ¼ cup oil in a blender or food processor fitted with the metal blade and purée. With the motor running, gradually add enough oil to form a thick, emulsified sauce. Season with salt and pepper.

The pesto may be stored, covered, in the refrigerator for up to 1 week, or frozen for longer storage.

Grilled Veal Chops with Billy's Mother's Caponata Relish

SERVES 4

2 tablespoons crushed garlic
1/2 teaspoon crushed fresh
rosemary
1/2 teaspoon freshly ground
black pepper

1/2 teaspoon salt
4 twelve-ounce veal chops
Billy's Mother's Caponata
Relish (see recipe below)

In a small bowl, blend the garlic, rosemary, pepper, and salt into a paste. Rub into the veal chops and let sit at room temperature for 2 hours.

Prepare a charcoal or gas grill for cooking.

Place the chops in the center of the hot grill and sear quickly on both sides to seal in the juices. Move to a cooler spot on the grill and cook, turning once, for about 4 minutes, or until medium rare. (The chops may also be roasted in a preheated 350-degree oven for 10 to 15 minutes.)

Place one chop on each of four warm serving plates. Serve immediately with Billy's Mother's Caponata Relish and French bread toasted with Garlic Spread (see page 183) passed separately.

Billy's Mother's Caponata Relish
MAKES 6 CUPS

1/2 cup olive oil
4 tomatoes, peeled, seeded, and chopped
1/2 yellow onion, peeled and minced
1 tablespoon minced garlic
Pinch of dried basil
Pinch of dried oregano
1 large eggplant, peeled and finely chopped
Salt to taste
5 celery stalks, trimmed and finely chopped
1 cup green olives, drained, pitted, and finely chopped
1 cup toasted pine nuts
1/3 cup red wine vinegar
1/3 cup sugar
Freshly ground black pepper to taste

Heat 1/4 cup oil in a heavy saucepan over high heat. Add the tomatoes, onion, garlic, and herbs. Lower the heat and sauté for 15 to 20 minutes. Remove from the heat and set aside.

Sprinkle the eggplant with 4 tablespoons salt, toss, and let sit at room temperature for 20 minutes.

Fill a small pot with water, bring to a boil, and add the celery to blanch. Remove and refresh under cold running water. Drain and pat dry. Repeat the process with the olives. Fold the celery and olives into the tomato mixture.

Thoroughly rinse the salt from the eggplant under cold running water. Drain on paper towels. Heat the remaining 1/4 cup oil in a clean skillet over high heat. Add the eggplant and sauté for 2 minutes, or until tender. Fold the pine nuts into the eggplant. Remove the mixture from the heat and set aside to cool. Combine the eggplant mixture with the tomato mixture.

In a small saucepan over medium heat, combine the vinegar, sugar, and 1/3 cup water. Cook for 3 minutes, or until the sugar dissolves. Remove from the heat and set aside to cool.

Stir the vinegar-sugar mixture into the caponata a bit at a time, until the desired consistency is reached. The caponata should remain thick, like a relish. Adjust the seasoning with salt and pepper and refrigerate until ready to use.

The caponata can be made ahead and stored, covered, in the refrigerator.

Roulade of Veal with Spinach, Pine Nuts, and Crabmeat, and Marsala Sauce

SERVES 4

2 eight-ounce veal loins, completely trimmed of fat and sinew
Salt to taste
Freshly ground black pepper to taste
1/4 cup Clarified Butter (see page 180) or vegetable oil
1/4 cup Pernod
4 shallots, peeled and minced
2 cloves garlic, peeled and minced
Pinch of nutmeg

1/4 pound fresh lump crabmeat, picked over to remove any shell and cartilage
1/2 pound spinach, thoroughly rinsed in salted water, blanched, drained, and chopped
1/2 cup pine nuts, toasted and cooled
Vegetable oil
Marsala Sauce (see recipe below)

Butterfly each veal loin by running a thin, sharp knife horizontally almost but not all the way through the thickness of the meat, so the loin hinges open at one end. Spread the meat open and sprinkle lightly with water. Gently pound with a meat mallet to double the area of the loin. Season with salt and pepper and set aside.

Heat the butter in a heavy sauté pan over medium-high heat. Add the Pernod, shallots, garlic, and nutmeg and sauté for 2 minutes, or until the shallots are translucent. Add the crabmeat and spinach and mix well. Fold in the pine nuts and season with salt and pepper. Remove from the heat and set aside to cool.

Preheat the oven to 325 degrees.

Spread half of the spinach-crabmeat mixture on each loin, leaving a ½-inch border all around. Beginning at one end, roll each loin tightly and secure with toothpicks. Brush lightly with oil, place in a roasting pan in the preheated oven, and roast for 15 minutes.

Remove from the oven and let sit for 5 minutes, then slice into ½-inch rounds.

Lightly coat four warm serving plates with Marsala Sauce. Arrange an equal number of veal slices on each plate on top of the sauce and serve immediately.

Marsala Sauce
MAKES 2 CUPS

1 stick (½ cup) plus 2 teaspoons unsalted butter
2 shallots, peeled and finely chopped
½ cup Marsala
¾ cup Demi-Glace (see page 171)
Salt to taste
Freshly ground black pepper to taste

Heat 2 teaspoons butter in a small saucepan over medium heat. Add the shallots and sauté for 2 minutes or until translucent. Add the Marsala and cook for 5 minutes, or until reduced by half. Add the demi-glace and simmer for 1 minute. Remove from the heat and fold in the remaining ½ cup butter. Strain the sauce and season with salt and pepper. Keep warm until ready to serve.

Roast Tenderloin of Beef with Creole Cardinal Sauce

SERVES 4

2 *pounds center-cut beef*
   tenderloin
   Salt to taste
   Freshly ground black pepper
   to taste
¹/₄ *cup vegetable oil*
¹/₄ *cup minced shallots*
¹/₂ *cup Madeira or dry sherry*
¹/₄ *cup heavy cream*

2 *cups Lobster Sauce (see*
   page 178)
¹/₂ *pound cooked crawfish tail*
   meat, tails intact
2 *tablespoons snipped fresh*
   chives
1 *teaspoon diced black truffle*
   (optional)

Preheat the oven to 350 degrees.

Season the tenderloin with salt and pepper and brush with the oil. Heat a heavy skillet over high heat. Add the beef and quickly sear on all sides. Remove from the skillet. Set the skillet aside; do not discard the fat. Place the tenderloin on a rack in a roasting pan in the preheated oven and roast for 15 to 20 minutes for medium rare (or longer, according to your preference). Remove the meat from the oven, cover, and keep warm.

Reheat the oil in the skillet over medium heat. Add the shallots and sauté for 2 minutes, or until tender. Add the Madeira, stirring constantly to deglaze the pan. Add the cream and Lobster Sauce and bring to a boil. Season with salt and pepper and strain into a clean saucepan.

Fold the crawfish tails, chives, truffle, and any juices drained from the tenderloin into the sauce and adjust the seasoning with salt and pepper. Place over low heat for 2 minutes just to heat through.

Slice the tenderloin into eight equal slices. Place two slices on each of four warm serving plates and spoon the sauce over the meat. Serve immediately. You may also pass the sauce separately if you prefer.

Tournedos of Beef with Red Butter and Beef Marrow

SERVES 4

8 ounces beef marrowbone (have your butcher cut the bone into 8 slices)
4 one-and-a-half-inch-thick 6-ounce beef tournedos (from the thick end of the tenderloin)
Salt to taste
Freshly ground black pepper to taste

¼ cup Clarified Butter (see page 180) or vegetable oil
8 shallots, peeled and sliced into thin rings
Sprig of fresh thyme
1 bay leaf
1 cup red wine
2 tablespoons Demi-Glace (see page 171)
2 sticks (1 cup) unsalted butter

Push out the marrow from the bones with your fingers. Soak the slices of marrow in ice water to remove any blood.

Tie a piece of kitchen string around the girth of each tournedo to help retain moisture during cooking. Season with salt and pepper.

Heat the clarified butter in a heavy skillet over high heat. Add the tournedos and sear on all sides. Lower the heat to medium and cook for 2 minutes on each side, or until just rare. Remove from the pan and keep warm.

Add the shallots, thyme, and bay leaf to the pan and sauté for 2 minutes, or until the shallots are tender. Remove the mixture from the pan using a slotted spoon. Discard the thyme and bay leaf and reserve the shallots. Pour off any remaining fat from the pan. Return to medium heat and add the wine, stirring constantly to deglaze. Add the demi-glace and cook until reduced by half. Return the shallots to the pan and cook for 1 minute, or just until the mixture is warmed through. Remove from the heat and whisk in the butter, a bit at a time. Keep warm until ready to serve.

Preheat the broiler.

Remove the string from the tournedos. Drain the beef marrow and place two pieces on top of each filet. Place the tournedos on a baking sheet under the preheated broiler and broil for 30 seconds, or until the marrow becomes soft. Immediately remove from the broiler and sprinkle with coarsely ground black pepper.

Place one tournedo on each of four warm serving plates and surround with the sauce. Serve immediately.

IX SIDE DISHES AND VEGETABLES

Potato Terrine

Creole Potatoes Dauphine

Rosemary Baked Potatoes

Vegetable Terrine

Cheese-Battered Tomatoes

Creole Ratatouille

Stuffed Squash Blossoms

Cilantro and Turmeric Pilaf

Quick Mushroom Soufflé

Potato Terrine

SERVES 4

2 *large baking potatoes, rinsed and peeled*
4 *large eggs*
³/₄ *cup heavy cream*
¹/₃ *cup grated Parmesan cheese*

¹/₂ *teaspoon grated nutmeg*
¹/₂ *teaspoon salt*
¹/₂ *teaspoon freshly ground white pepper*
3 *ounces Swiss cheese, grated*

Slice the potatoes into ¹/₈-inch-thick rounds. Fill a large bowl with cold water, add the potato slices, and let sit for 30 minutes.

Preheat the oven to 375 degrees.

Drain the potatoes and dry on paper towels. Place in a single layer on a baking sheet and bake in the preheated oven for about 17 minutes, or just until tender. Do not turn off the oven.

In a medium bowl, combine the eggs, cream, Parmesan, nutmeg, salt, and pepper and blend thoroughly. Grease a 1¹/₂-quart soufflé dish or loaf pan. Beginning and ending with the potato slices, fill with alternating layers of potatoes and Swiss cheese.

Pour the egg mixture over the potatoes. Place in the preheated oven and bake for 25 minutes. Remove from the oven, set aside to cool, then invert and unmold. Slice into wedges or squares.

To serve hot, either microwave for 30 seconds or wrap in foil and place in a preheated 375-degree oven for about 10 minutes.

Creole Potatoes Dauphine

SERVES 4

1 stick (½ cup) unsalted
　butter
½ heaping cup sifted all-
　purpose flour
2 large eggs, beaten
　Salt to taste
2 pounds baking potatoes

2 large egg yolks
　Pinch of grated nutmeg
2 teaspoons Windsor Court
　Pepper (see page 189)
　Freshly ground white pepper
　to taste
1 quart vegetable oil

In a heavy saucepan over high heat, combine ½ cup water and ½ stick butter and bring to a boil. Remove from the heat and stir in the sifted flour, mixing well with a wooden spoon. Return to medium heat and stir continuously until the mixture pulls away from the side of the pan. Remove from the heat and let cool slightly, then beat in the beaten eggs and a pinch of salt. Cover and set aside.

Fill a large pot with salted water and bring to a boil. Rinse and peel the potatoes and cut them evenly into ⅛-inch-thick rounds. Drop them into the boiling water and cook, covered, for about 17 minutes, or until easily pierced with a fork. Drain well and return to the pot. Cover and return briefly to medium-high heat to dry any moisture, shaking gently to prevent sticking. Remove from the heat and transfer to the bowl of an electric mixer. Whip slowly, adding the egg yolks, the remaining ½ stick butter, the nutmeg, peppers, and salt. Test the consistency by pressing two fingers flat onto the mixture; if it is correct, your fingers will come away clean. If not, while the mixture is hot, spread it thinly on a baking sheet to allow as much moisture to evaporate as possible.

Combine the flour and potato mixtures and form into balls or quenelles about 1 tablespoon in size.

Heat the oil to 375 degrees in a deep-sided saucepan. Add the potato balls, a few at a time, and fry until golden brown. Remove with a slotted spoon, drain on paper towels, and keep warm until all the balls have been fried. Serve immediately.

The potato balls may be formed and frozen, uncooked, for later use. Defrost thoroughly before frying.

Rosemary Baked Potatoes

SERVES 4

4 baking potatoes
4 sprigs fresh rosemary (*thyme may be substituted*)

1 pound rock salt

Preheat the oven to 375 degrees.

Wash and dry the potatoes. With a metal or wooden skewer, pierce the potatoes all the way through, lengthwise. With a sharp knife, sharpen the rosemary branches to a point. Push the rosemary into the holes made by the skewer.

Spread a layer of rock salt over the surface of a shallow baking dish large enough to accommodate all the potatoes in one layer. Set the potatoes on the salt, making sure that their sides are not touching. Bake in the preheated oven for 45 minutes to 1 hour, or until easily pierced with a fork.

Remove the potatoes from the oven and pull out the rosemary skewers. Serve hot with grilled meat or fish.

Vegetable Terrine

MAKES ONE 10- BY
4- BY 4-INCH LOAF

3 medium carrots
1 eggplant
1 pound asparagus tips
1 large zucchini
2 medium yellow squash
1 large whole tomato
1 large red bell pepper

8 shiitake mushroom caps,
  rinsed and dried
  Salt to taste
  Freshly ground white pepper
  to taste
1 cup olive oil
4 teaspoons unflavored gelatin

Trim and peel the carrots. Peel the eggplant. Rinse and dry the asparagus tips, zucchini, yellow squash, tomato, and red pepper. Trim the stem ends of the squash and core the tomato.

Fill a medium pot with water, add a pinch of salt, and bring to a boil. Slice the carrots lengthwise, paper thin. Blanch the carrots and then the asparagus in the boiling water. Refresh under cold running water. Pat dry and set aside, each on a separate plate.

Slice the zucchini, squash, eggplant, and tomato into rounds. Cut the pepper in half. Stem, seed, and then remove the white membrane from the inside, and slice into flat pieces 2 to 3 inches wide. Season all of the vegetables, including the mushrooms, with salt and pepper.

Place the oil in a large, heavy skillet and heat until almost smoking. Add each vegetable except the carrots and asparagus, one variety at a time. Sauté each for about 15 seconds, then remove with a slotted spoon. Do not overcook. The quick-fry simply brings out the color of the vegetables.

Line a 10- by 4- by 4-inch terrine with plastic wrap and arrange slices of carrot along the bottom and up the sides, slightly overlapping. Fill the terrine with layers of squash, mushrooms, zucchini, tomato, asparagus, red pepper, and eggplant.

Heat 1 cup water in a small saucepan and sprinkle the gelatin over the surface. Let soften, then warm over low heat until completely dissolved.

Pour the gelatin over the vegetables and fold the carrot slices from the sides over the top to seal the top. Cover the terrine with plastic wrap and set another pan filled with water on top to press the vegetables down and make the terrine firm. (The weight of the pan will expel any excess gelatin.) Refrigerate for 12 hours.

To unmold, remove the top pan and top layer of plastic wrap, then dip the terrine in hot water for 10 seconds. Invert onto a serving platter. Remove the remaining plastic wrap and slice, keeping one thumb on top of the terrine and a hand on the cut end to keep it intact. Serve cold.

Cheese-Battered Tomatoes

SERVES 4

2 large eggs
¼ cup grated Parmesan cheese
1 tablespoon finely chopped
    fresh basil
2 large tomatoes

½ cup all-purpose flour
    Salt to taste
    Freshly ground black pepper
    to taste
¼ cup olive oil

In a medium bowl, beat the eggs, then fold in the Parmesan and basil. Let sit for 30 minutes at room temperature.

Slice off both ends of the tomatoes and discard. Cut each tomato into four rounds of equal thickness. Season the flour with salt and pepper.

Heat the olive oil in a heavy skillet over medium-high heat. Dust the tomato slices on both sides with the seasoned flour, then dip into the egg mixture. Place the tomatoes in the skillet and sauté, turning once, until golden brown. Drain on paper towels.

Serve hot as a vegetable with meats, or as an appetizer with angel hair pasta.

Creole Ratatouille

SERVES 6 TO 8

½ cup olive oil
1 yellow onion, peeled and finely chopped
4 cloves garlic, peeled and finely chopped
2 small zucchini, trimmed and cut into ¼-inch dice
½ medium green bell pepper, seeded and finely chopped
½ medium red bell pepper, seeded and finely chopped
½ teaspoon dried thyme
1 pound eggplant, peeled and cut into ¼-inch dice

2 large very ripe tomatoes, peeled, cored, seeded, and finely chopped (if very ripe tomatoes are unavailable, 16 ounces canned, well-drained plum tomatoes can be substituted)
¼ cup white wine
½ teaspoon Windsor Court Pepper (see page 189)
2 bay leaves
Salt to taste
Freshly ground black pepper to taste

Heat the oil in a large skillet over medium heat. When hot, add the onion, garlic, zucchini, bell peppers, and thyme. Sauté for 2 minutes, or until the onion is soft, then add the eggplant. Cook for another 2 minutes. Stir in the tomatoes, wine, Windsor Court Pepper, and bay leaves. Sauté for another 5 minutes. Adjust the seasoning with salt and pepper. Remove from the heat and serve hot.

Stuffed Squash Blossoms

MAKES 12

1 large egg
1½ cups all-purpose flour
   Salt to taste
2 tablespoons olive oil
1 yellow onion, peeled and
   finely chopped
1 red bell pepper, cored,
   seeded, and finely chopped
1 small eggplant, cut into ½-
   inch cubes

2 tomatoes, peeled, cored,
   seeded, and chopped
2 cloves garlic, peeled and
   finely chopped
   Freshly ground black pepper
   to taste
12 squash blossoms
1 quart vegetable oil

In a medium bowl, beat the egg with 1 cup cold water until well blended. Gently stir in 1 cup flour and a pinch of salt. Set aside.

Heat the oil in a skillet over medium heat. Add the onion and sauté for 2 minutes, or until tender. Remove from the pan with a slotted spoon and set aside. Add the red pepper, eggplant, tomatoes, and garlic to the pan and sauté for about 5 minutes, or until soft. Stir the onion back into the skillet with the other vegetables. Season with salt and pepper. Lower the heat and simmer for 10 minutes. Remove from the heat and set aside to cool.

Place the cooled vegetable mixture in a pastry bag fitted

with a plain ½-inch tube. Pipe the mixture into the squash blossoms and press the edges of the petals to seal closed.

In a large skillet, heat 3 inches of oil to 350 degrees on a candy thermometer. Gently roll the squash blossoms in the remaining ½ cup flour, then dip into the reserved batter. Place in the hot oil, a few at a time, and fry for 3 to 5 minutes, turning to brown evenly. Remove from the oil and drain well on paper towels. Season with salt and pepper. Serve hot.

Cilantro and Turmeric Pilaf

SERVES 4

*½ stick (¼ cup) unsalted
   butter
1 cup long-grain rice
2 tablespoons finely chopped
   shallots
1 clove garlic, peeled and
   minced
1 teaspoon ground turmeric*

*1 bay leaf
¾ cup Chicken Stock (see
   page 169)
¼ cup chopped cilantro (or to
   taste)
Salt to taste
Freshly ground black pepper
   to taste*

Preheat the oven to 400 degrees.

Melt the butter in a heavy ovenproof saucepan over medium heat. Add the rice, shallots, and garlic and sauté for 2 minutes, or until the rice becomes glassy. Stir in the turmeric, bay leaf, and chicken stock. Raise the heat and bring to a boil. Remove from the heat.

Cover, place in the preheated oven, and bake for about 20 minutes, or until the rice is tender. Fold in the cilantro, season with salt and pepper, and serve immediately.

Quick Mushroom Soufflé

SERVES 4

¼ cup Clarified Butter (see page 180) or vegetable oil
¼ pound button mushrooms, rinsed, dried, and quartered
¼ pound chanterelle mushrooms, rinsed, dried, and quartered*
⅛ pound morel mushrooms, sliced*
1 shallot, peeled and finely chopped

Pinch of dried thyme
Salt to taste
Freshly ground black pepper to taste
½ cup Béchamel Sauce, at room temperature (see page 175)
½ cup grated Parmesan cheese
2 large egg whites

Preheat the oven to 325 degrees.

Generously butter one 1-quart or four ½-cup soufflé molds. Dust the insides with flour. Set aside.

Heat the butter in a large skillet over medium-high heat. Add all of the mushrooms, the shallot, and the thyme and sauté for 2 minutes, or until the shallot is soft. Season with salt and pepper. Place the mushroom mixture in a strainer over a bowl and let sit for 5 minutes. Reserve the liquid that collects in

* An equivalent quantity of any fresh mushrooms may be substituted.

the bowl. Set the mushrooms aside in the strainer, allowing any liquid to continue to drain off.

Return the reserved liquid to the pan and cook over high heat for 5 minutes, or until thick enough to glaze a spoon. Remove from the heat and set aside.

In a medium bowl, combine the béchamel sauce and Parmesan. Whip the egg whites to stiff peaks. Toss the mushrooms in the mushroom glaze and place in the bottom of the 1-quart mold or divide equally among the four $1/2$-cup molds. Fold the egg whites gently into the cheese sauce and pour over the mushrooms. Clean any drips from the sides of the molds.

Place in the preheated oven and bake for 15 minutes.

Serve immediately.

SAUCES AND STOCKS

Chicken Stock

Fish Stock

Demi-Glace

Beurre Blanc #1

Beurre Blanc #2

Béchamel Sauce

Hollandaise Sauce

Lobster Sauce

Clarified Butter

Red Onion Confiture

Spiced Glazing Butter

Garlic Spread

Tabasco-Mint Compound Butter

Tomatoes Concassé

Tomato-Caper Relish

Tri-color Relish

Harvey's Curry Powder

Windsor Court Pepper

Egg Wash

Chicken Stock

MAKES 3 QUARTS

4 pounds chicken bones
2 white onions, peeled and
  finely chopped
2 bay leaves
1/2 head celery, trimmed and
  finely chopped

2 leeks, white part only,
  thoroughly rinsed and
  finely chopped
10–12 white peppercorns

Combine all the ingredients in a large stock pot. Add 1 gallon of water. Bring the mixture to a boil over high heat, skimming any scum that forms on the surface. Lower the heat and simmer, uncovered, for 1 hour, skimming any additional scum that forms on the surface.

Strain and cool. The stock may be stored, covered, in the refrigerator for up to 1 week, or frozen in small portions for longer storage.

Fish Stock

MAKES 2 QUARTS

2 pounds fish bones from lean white fish such as sole, flounder, grouper, bass, or drum
1 stick (½ cup) unsalted butter
1 white onion, peeled and chopped

1 leek, white part only, thoroughly rinsed and chopped
4 stalks celery, trimmed and finely chopped
6 white peppercorns
1 bay leaf
2 cups white wine

Rinse the fish bones under cold running water. Melt the butter in a large stock pot over medium heat. Add the fish bones, onion, leek, celery, peppercorns, and bay leaf and sauté for 4 minutes, or until onion is tender.

Add the wine and 2 quarts of water. Raise the heat and bring to a rolling boil. Reduce the heat and simmer for 20 minutes, skimming often to remove any scum that forms on the surface.

Strain and cool. The stock may be stored, covered, in the refrigerator for up to 2 days, or frozen in small portions for longer storage.

Demi-Glace*

MAKES 2 GALLONS

4 *pounds chicken bones*
1 *pound beef or veal bones*
½ *cup peanut oil or*
  vegetable oil
2 *leeks, white part only,*
  thoroughly rinsed and
  chopped
2 *large onions, peeled and*
  roughly chopped
2 *small bulbs garlic, peeled*
  and roughly chopped

2 *large carrots, peeled and*
  roughly chopped
1 *head celery, trimmed and*
  roughly chopped
2 *tablespoons dried thyme*
1 *tablespoon dried rosemary*
1 *tablespoon dried marjoram*
2 *bay leaves*
2 *cups tomato paste*
4 *cups red wine*
¼ *cup arrowroot (optional)*

Preheat the oven to 400 degrees.

Place the chicken and beef or veal bones in a roasting pan and place in the preheated oven. Roast for 15 minutes, or until well browned. Fill a large stock pot with 3 gallons of water and bring to a boil over high heat. Add the browned bones. Return to a boil, then reduce the heat to medium and let simmer. Place the roasting pan over high heat. Add ½ cup boiling water and stir to deglaze the pan. Add the resulting juices to the stock pot.

* This is not a true demi-glace, but one that can be easily prepared in the home kitchen.

Heat the oil in a large skillet over high heat. Add the leeks, onions, garlic, carrots, celery, thyme, rosemary, marjoram, and bay leaves. Sauté for 4 minutes, or until the onions are tender. Reduce the heat to low and add the tomato paste, stirring constantly until the mixture caramelizes and turns brown. Add the wine and stir well, scraping any residue off the bottom of the pan.

Add the vegetable mixture to the bones and water and place over medium heat. Bring to a simmer and cook, uncovered, for about 2 hours, or until the amount of liquid has reduced by half. Strain into a clean saucepan and check the consistency. The stock should be thick enough to glaze a spoon. If too thin, continue to reduce, or mix the arrowroot with a little cooled stock and gradually whisk into the stock until the desired thickness is reached.

Pour into 1-cup containers and cover. Refrigerate for up to 3 days, or freeze for longer storage.

Beurre Blanc #1

MAKES 3 CUPS

2 tablespoons Clarified
  Butter (*see page 180*) *or*
  vegetable oil
3 shallots, peeled and roughly
  chopped
1 bay leaf
1/2 teaspoon black peppercorns
1/4 cup white wine
2 tablespoons champagne
  vinegar or white wine
  vinegar

1/4 cup heavy cream
4 sticks (1 pound) unsalted
  butter, softened
  Salt to taste
  Freshly ground white pepper
  to taste

Heat the clarified butter in a small heavy saucepan over medium heat. Add the shallots, bay leaf, and peppercorns and
sauté for 2 minutes. Add the wine and vinegar and continue to
cook for 7 minutes, or until the liquid is reduced to 1 tablespoon. Stir in the heavy cream. Raise the heat and bring to a
rolling boil for 2 minutes. Remove from the heat and whisk in
the butter, a piece at a time. Strain and season with salt and
pepper. Keep warm in a container over warm water until ready
to use.

Beurre Blanc #2

MAKES 3 CUPS

6 sticks (1½ pounds) unsalted
 butter, softened
2 shallots, peeled and roughly
 chopped
1 bay leaf
2 tablespoons freshly squeezed
 lemon juice

2 tablespoons white wine
 vinegar
 Pinch of freshly ground
 white pepper
½ cup dry white wine

Heat 4 tablespoons butter in a nonreactive saucepan over medium heat. Add the shallots and bay leaf and sauté for 2 minutes, or until the shallots are soft and translucent. Add the lemon juice, vinegar, pepper, and wine and cook for 5 minutes, or until the liquid is reduced by half. Lower the heat and whisk in the remaining butter, a piece at a time, being careful not to overheat or the mixture will separate. Strain. Keep warm in a container over warm water until ready to use.

Béchamel Sauce

MAKES 4 CUPS

5 cups milk
1 small yellow onion, peeled
1 bay leaf
1 whole clove
1 stick (1/2 cup) unsalted butter

1/2 cup all-purpose flour
Salt to taste
Freshly ground white pepper
to taste

In a heavy saucepan over high heat, combine the milk, onion, bay leaf, and clove. Bring to a boil. Reduce the heat and simmer for 5 minutes. Cover, remove from the heat, and set aside.

Melt the butter in a medium saucepan over medium heat. When foamy, whisk in the flour and cook for 1 minute, making sure the mixture does not burn.

Remove from the heat and strain the warm milk into the flour mixture, whisking continuously until smooth. Return to medium heat and bring to a gentle boil, again whisking continuously to prevent lumps. As the sauce thickens, lower the heat and simmer for 2 minutes to cook out the taste of the flour. Strain. Season with salt and pepper.

When cool, the sauce may be stored, covered, in the refrigerator for up to 1 week, or frozen in small portions for 2 to 3 months.

Hollandaise Sauce

MAKES 2 CUPS

8 white peppercorns, crushed
1 shallot, peeled and finely
  chopped
2 tablespoons champagne
  vinegar or white wine
  vinegar

1 tablespoon white wine
3 large egg yolks
  Salt to taste
  Cayenne pepper to taste
1 cup Clarified Butter (see page
  180), warmed

Combine the peppercorns, shallot, and vinegar in a small, heavy saucepan over high heat. Bring to a boil and cook for 3 minutes, or until the liquid is reduced by half. Add the wine and remove from the heat. Let sit, at room temperature, until the mixture is just warm.

Combine the egg yolks with a pinch of salt and cayenne pepper in the top half of a double boiler. Strain the wine mixture into the yolks, then place over simmering water. Whip with a fine wire whisk until thoroughly combined. Continue to whisk for about 5 minutes, or until the mixture turns pale yellow and thickens. To avoid overcooking the egg yolks, occasionally remove from the heat.

When the yolk mixture is the consistency of whipped cream, remove from the heat and slowly whisk in the clarified butter.

If the sauce should curdle while adding the butter, let cool for 5 minutes. Place 2 tablespoons boiling water in a clean bowl and slowly whisk in the broken sauce, then continue adding the clarified butter.

Adjust the seasoning with salt and cayenne pepper. Keep warm in a container over warm water until ready to use.

Lobster Sauce

MAKES 2 QUARTS

2 one-pound lobsters*
¼ cup Clarified Butter (see page 180)
4 shallots, peeled and roughly chopped
½ cup loosely packed fresh tarragon leaves
2 cloves garlic, peeled and finely chopped
2 bay leaves
1 small carrot, peeled and chopped
2 leeks, white part only, thoroughly rinsed and chopped

¼ cup brandy
¼ cup Madeira
1 cup all-purpose flour
½ cup tomato paste
2 quarts Fish Stock (see page 170)
10 white peppercorns
2 cups heavy cream
Salt to taste
Freshly ground black pepper to taste

Using a sharp knife, pierce through the shell and flesh of each live lobster at the cross-shaped mark behind the lobster's head. Split the lobster in half lengthwise and twist off the legs and

* This recipe works equally well with steamed lobsters. Use the shell and carcass, along with any juices rendered during cooking, in the sauce. Refrigerate or freeze the claw and tail meat for later use.

claws. Remove the claw and tail meat and refrigerate or freeze for later use. Remove and discard the semitranslucent sac found inside the head on both sides. Reserve the greenish tomalley (liver) and any roe. Crack the shells and chop the carcass into large pieces.

In a large, heavy saucepan over medium heat, heat the clarified butter almost until smoking. Add all the lobster, including any tomalley and roe, the shallots, tarragon, garlic, bay leaves, carrot, and leeks. Raise the heat and cook for 3 minutes, or until the lobster turns bright pink. Pour the brandy over the lobster and flame, then add the Madeira. Stir in the flour and tomato paste. When well blended and hot, add the fish stock and peppercorns and bring to a boil. Lower the heat to a simmer and cook for 1 hour, or until the liquid is reduced by half. Strain into a clean pot. Place over medium heat and add the cream. Cook for 5 minutes, or until the sauce thickens. Adjust the seasoning with salt and pepper and, if desired, strain again.

Lobster Sauce may be stored, covered, in the refrigerator for 2 days, or frozen in individual containers for longer storage.

Clarified Butter

MAKES 2 TO 3 CUPS   *8 sticks (2 pounds) unsalted*
butter

In the top half of a double boiler over simmering water, slowly melt the butter so that the solids separate from the fat. Skim the clarified butter off the top with a ladle and refrigerate.

Clarified Butter may be stored, covered, in the refrigerator for up to 2 weeks, or frozen in small portions for longer storage.

It is possible to infuse many flavors into the butter during clarification. For example, crawfish butter can be made by adding shells and fat to the melting butter. Strain out the shells before storing. Use for sautéing fish.

To use for frying at high temperatures, combine 1 pound butter and 1 pound margarine and clarify as described above. Equal parts clarified butter and peanut oil work equally well.

The milky residue left from the clarification process can be used for sautéing vegetables such as carrots and potatoes.

Red Onion Confiture

MAKES 2 CUPS

¹/₂ stick (¹/₄ cup) unsalted butter
¹/₄ cup sugar
6 red onions, peeled and thinly sliced
2 tablespoons red wine vinegar

2 tablespoons red wine
Salt to taste
Freshly ground black pepper to taste
1¹/₂ teaspoons grenadine syrup

Melt the butter in a large deep-sided sauté pan over medium heat. Add the sugar and cook, stirring constantly, for 10 minutes, or until the mixture caramelizes and turns light brown. Add the sliced onions, vinegar, wine, and 1 tablespoon water. Cover and cook, stirring occasionally, for about 15 minutes, or until the onions are soft. Season with salt and pepper. Remove from the heat and stir in the grenadine.

Serve warm or cold as an accompaniment to any grilled meat or fish.

This dish can be made up to 1 day ahead and stored, covered, in the refrigerator.

Spiced Glazing Butter

MAKES 4 CUPS

4 sticks (1 pound) unsalted
  butter, softened
3 large eggs
2 teaspoons Harvey's Curry
  Powder (see page 188)
¼ cup tomato ketchup
½ teaspoon ground dried thyme
½ teaspoon ground dried
  marjoram
½ teaspoon dried rosemary,
  crumbled

½ teaspoon dried tarragon,
  crumbled
6 anchovy fillets, minced
½ teaspoon freshly ground
  black pepper
¼ cup Demi-Glace (see page
  171)
2 tablespoons chopped fresh
  parsley

With an electric mixer on high speed, whip the butter until
almost white. Add the remaining ingredients and beat for 1
minute, scraping the sides of the bowl.

Divide the mixture in half and spread each portion onto a
sheet of plastic wrap or wax paper. Roll into a log, wrap tightly,
and refrigerate or freeze.

Slice and use to flavor grilled meats, game, or poultry. For
grilled or broiled steaks, place ¼-inch slices of Spiced Glazing
Butter on the meat during the last minute or two of cooking.

Garlic Spread

MAKES 1 CUP

1 stick (¹/₂ cup) unsalted
  butter, softened
2 tablespoons olive oil
2 tablespoons puréed garlic
¹/₄ cup chopped fresh parsley
  Pinch of dried basil

¹/₄ cup grated Parmesan cheese
1¹/₂ teaspoons Worcestershire
  sauce
¹/₄ teaspoon freshly ground
  black pepper

Combine all the ingredients in a small bowl and stir to blend thoroughly.

Use as a spread on a split loaf of French bread that has been baked or broiled until warm and toasty, on baked or grilled vegetables, or on pasta.

Garlic Spread may be stored, well covered, in the refrigerator for up to 1 month.

Tabasco-Mint Compound Butter

MAKES 2 CUPS

2 tablespoons Clarified
   Butter (see page 180) or
   vegetable oil
2 shallots, peeled and finely
   minced
4 sticks (1 pound) unsalted
   butter, softened

2 large egg yolks
6 teaspoons Tabasco sauce
2 teaspoons finely chopped fresh
   mint leaves

Heat the clarified butter in a small sauté pan over medium heat. Add the shallots and sauté for 3 minutes, or until soft. Remove from the heat and let cool to room temperature.

With an electric mixer on high speed, whip the softened butter until almost white. Add the cooled shallots, egg yolks, Tabasco, and mint leaves and beat for 30 seconds, scraping the sides of the bowl.

Divide the mixture in half and spread each portion onto a sheet of plastic wrap or wax paper. Roll into a log, wrap tightly, and refrigerate or freeze.

Slice and use to flavor grilled meats, fish, or shellfish.

Tomatoes Concassé

MAKES 2 CUPS

2 tablespoons Clarified Butter
(see page 180)
4 shallots, peeled and chopped
2 cloves garlic, peeled and finely
chopped
1 bay leaf
1 sprig fresh thyme

6 tomatoes, cored, peeled,
seeded, and diced
½ cup white wine
Salt to taste
Freshly ground black pepper
to taste

Heat the clarified butter in a skillet over medium heat. Add the shallots, garlic, bay leaf, and thyme and sauté for 2 minutes, or until the shallots are tender. Add the tomatoes and stir to blend. Sauté for an additional 10 minutes, then add the wine and stir to deglaze the pan. Continue cooking for about 10 minutes, or until the liquid is reduced by half. Season with salt and pepper.

Remove from the heat and discard the thyme sprig. Let cool to room temperature. Tomatoes Concassé may be stored, covered, in the refrigerator for up to 1 week.

Use concassé as a base for other sauces. You may substitute tarragon, basil, oregano, or other fresh herbs for the thyme in this recipe.

Tomato-Caper Relish

MAKES 1 QUART

¹/₄ cup olive oil
4 cups peeled, cored, seeded, and finely chopped tomatoes
¹/₂ cup finely chopped red onion
2 tablespoons minced fresh gingerroot

4 cloves garlic, peeled and finely chopped
¹/₄ cup capers, rinsed and drained
1 teaspoon salt
1 teaspoon freshly ground black pepper

Heat the oil in a heavy saucepan over medium heat. Add the tomatoes, onion, ginger, and garlic. Sauté for 15 minutes, or until the mixture has reduced by half. Add the capers, salt, and pepper and cook for another 2 minutes. Remove from the heat and let cool to room temperature.

Place in an airtight container and refrigerate for at least 8 hours before serving. This relish will keep, covered, in the refrigerator for several days.

Serve with smoked brook trout or other seafood dishes. For a spicier relish, add a dash of hot sauce before serving.

Tri-color Relish

MAKES 2 CUPS

1 cup finely chopped red bell
  pepper
1 cup finely chopped green bell
  pepper
1 cup finely chopped yellow bell
  pepper
1 fresh jalapeño pepper,
  stemmed, seeded, and finely
  chopped

1 tablespoon salt
1 cup finely chopped red
  onion
2 cups apple cider vinegar
1½ cups sugar
1 cup light corn syrup

Mix the peppers and salt in a large glass bowl and let sit at room temperature for 3 hours.

In a heavy saucepan over high heat, combine the peppers and their liquid with the onion, vinegar, sugar, and corn syrup. Bring to a boil. Lower the heat and simmer, stirring frequently, for about 1 hour, or until the onion is translucent and the mixture has thickened. Remove from the heat and let cool to room temperature.

Place in an airtight container and refrigerate for at least 8 hours before serving. This relish will keep, covered, in the refrigerator for up to 1 week.

Serve with cold meats such as thinly sliced roast beef or with grilled steak.

Harvey's Curry Powder

MAKES 1 CUP

2 tablespoons dry mustard
2 tablespoons ground
   coriander
2 tablespoons ground cashews
2 tablespoons ground
   turmeric

1½ teaspoons cayenne pepper
¼ cup ground cumin
2 tablespoons garlic powder
3 tablespoons paprika
¼ teaspoon ground cloves
¼ teaspoon ground cinnamon
¼ teaspoon ground cardamom

Combine all the ingredients in a small bowl and stir to blend thoroughly. Store in an airtight container at room temperature.

Windsor Court Pepper

MAKES 1 CUP

½ cup paprika
2 tablespoons cayenne pepper
2 tablespoons garlic powder
¼ teaspoon dried rosemary, crumbled
½ teaspoon dried thyme, crumbled
2 bay leaves, crumbled
¼ teaspoon salt (optional)

½ teaspoon freshly ground black pepper
½ teaspoon dried tarragon, crumbled
½ teaspoon dried basil, crumbled
2 tablespoons grated fresh lemon zest

In a blender or food processor fitted with the metal blade, combine all the ingredients and grind until thoroughly blended. Store in an airtight container at room temperature.

Egg Wash

1 cup milk

1 egg

Combine the milk and egg in a small bowl and whisk to blend. Strain into a container and cover. Egg Wash can be stored in the refrigerator for up to 3 days.

XI

BREAKFAST AND BRUNCH

Eggs Windsor Court

Scrambled Eggs
with Peppered Lobster

Omelette Linley

Pain Perdu

Pontchatoula Beignets
with Bourbon Whiskey Whipped Cream

Homemade Granola

Fresh Berries
in Champagne and Pastis

Bran Muffins

Berry-Nut Muffins

Currant Scones

Eggs Windsor Court

SERVES 4

¼ cup Clarified Butter (see page 180) or vegetable oil
6 ounces fresh mushrooms, rinsed, dried, and finely chopped
¼ cup minced shallots
Pinch of ground thyme
1 clove garlic, peeled and crushed
½ cup heavy cream
¼ cup white wine

Salt
Freshly ground black pepper
4 English muffins
2 tablespoons white wine vinegar
8 large eggs
8 thin slices smoked salmon
Tomato Béarnaise Sauce (see recipe below)
1 ounce Beluga caviar
1 ounce salmon caviar

Heat the clarified butter in a heavy saucepan over medium heat. Add the mushrooms, shallots, thyme, and garlic and sauté for about 5 minutes, or until all the rendered liquid has evaporated. Stir in the cream, the wine, and a pinch of salt and pepper. Lower the heat and simmer for about 4 minutes, or until the liquid has reduced and thickened. Remove from the heat and keep warm.

Split the English muffins and toast lightly. Set aside and keep warm.

Place 1 quart of water in a large, heavy saucepan over

medium-high heat and bring to a simmer. Add the vinegar and a pinch of salt to the water. With a spoon, stir to form a whirlpool in the water. Carefully crack the eggs one by one into the center of the whirlpool and poach for 3 minutes. Remove with a slotted spoon, drain on a cloth, and keep warm.

Spread the mushroom mixture on top of the toasted English muffin halves, and place two English muffin halves on each of four warm serving plates. Top each with a slice of salmon. Place a poached egg on top of the salmon and spoon Tomato Béarnaise Sauce over the eggs. Garnish one egg with Beluga caviar and the other with salmon caviar. Serve immediately.

Tomato Béarnaise Sauce
MAKES 2 CUPS

1 tablespoon Clarified Butter (see page 180) or vegetable oil
1 teaspoon chopped fresh tarragon
1 teaspoon tomato paste

1/4 cup seeded and finely chopped tomato
1 tablespoon chopped fresh parsley
2 cups Hollandaise Sauce (see page 176), warmed

Heat the clarified butter in a small skillet over medium heat. Add the tarragon and sauté for 1 minute. Lower the heat, stir in the tomato paste, and cook for 1 minute. Add the diced tomato and cook for 1 additional minute, then add the parsley. Stir to blend and let cool for 3 minutes. Fold into the warm hollandaise sauce. Keep warm until ready to use.

Scrambled Eggs with Peppered Lobster

SERVES 4

8 large eggs
2 tablespoons heavy cream
  Salt to taste
  Freshly ground white pepper
  to taste
2 tablespoons plus 2 teaspoons
  Clarified Butter (see page
  180) or light vegetable oil
8 ounces cooked lobster meat,
  finely chopped

1 teaspoon black peppercorns,
  roughly crushed
4 tablespoons brandy
1 cup Lobster Sauce (see
  page 178)
2 scallions, green part only,
  finely chopped

In a bowl, whisk the eggs, cream, salt, and white pepper together. Set aside.

Heat 2 tablespoons clarified butter in a small sauté pan over medium heat. Add the lobster meat and black peppercorns and sauté for 30 seconds. Add the brandy and quickly flame. Cover to extinguish the flame, then add the Lobster Sauce. Heat through, but do not boil, as overcooking will result in tough lobster. Remove from the heat and keep warm.

In an omelette pan or nonstick skillet, heat the remaining 2 teaspoons clarified butter over medium heat. Add the scallions and sauté for 30 seconds. Add the egg mixture and stir with a wooden spoon for 3 minutes, or until firm but not dry.

Divide the eggs equally among four warm serving plates. Spoon the Lobster Sauce alongside. Serve immediately with warm muffins, brioche, or croissants, and champagne.

Omelette Linley

SERVES 4

2 cups milk
1/2 stick (1/4 cup) unsalted
  butter
1/2 cup all-purpose flour
  Salt to taste
  Freshly ground black pepper
  to taste
1/2 cup heavy cream
1 1/2 cups grated Parmesan
  cheese

4 large egg yolks
1/2 cup Clarified Butter (see
  page 180) or vegetable oil
1 cup chopped red onion (or to
  taste)
8 ounces small smoked shrimp
  (available in gourmet or
  specialty food stores)
8 large eggs

Place the milk in a small saucepan over medium heat and bring to a boil. Remove from the heat and keep warm. Melt the butter in a heavy saucepan over medium heat. When foamy, whisk in the flour and cook, stirring constantly, for about 1 minute. Do not let the flour brown.

Whisk the hot milk into the flour mixture, stirring constantly, to form a smooth sauce. Lower the heat and cook for 1 to 2 minutes, or just until warmed through. Season with salt and pepper. Remove from the heat and keep warm.

Whip the cream until it forms stiff peaks. Combine with the

sauce, 1 cup Parmesan cheese, and the egg yolks and stir to blend. Season with salt and pepper and set aside.

Heat 2 tablespoons clarified butter in an omelette pan or 6-inch nonstick skillet. Add ¼ cup red onion and sauté for 2 minutes, or until soft. Add 2 ounces smoked shrimp and cook for 1 minute, or until warmed through. Beat 2 eggs and pour into the pan, stirring with a wooden spoon for approximately 30 seconds. Remove from the heat and let sit for an additional 30 seconds, or until a skin of cooked eggs forms on the bottom. The top of the eggs will still be soft.

Preheat the broiler.

Invert an ovenproof serving plate over the pan and turn the omelette out onto it. Keep warm while following the same procedure with the remaining ingredients to make 3 more omelettes.

Coat each omelette with the cheese sauce and sprinkle with the remaining ½ cup Parmesan cheese. Place under the preheated broiler and brown lightly. Serve immediately.

Pain Perdu

SERVES 4

6 large eggs
1 teaspoon pure vanilla extract
1 teaspoon orange blossom
  water
2 cups milk
1/2 cup brandy
3/4 cup sugar
  Grated zest of 1 lemon

1/2 cup sugarcane syrup (or
  blackstrap molasses)
1/4 cup pecan pieces
1 medium loaf day-old French
  bread
1/4 cup vegetable oil,
  approximately
1/4 cup confectioners' sugar

In a large bowl, whisk the eggs, vanilla, orange blossom water, and milk together. Set aside.

Warm the brandy in a small saucepan over medium heat. Ignite and flame, away from the heat. When the flames subside, return the pan to low heat and add the sugar and lemon zest. Cook, stirring constantly, for 3 minutes, or until the sugar dissolves. Remove from the heat and let cool, then stir into the egg mixture. Set aside.

Heat the cane syrup in a small pan over low heat. Add the pecans. Remove from the heat and keep warm.

Cut the French bread, diagonally, into 1-inch-thick rounds. Heat the oil in a heavy skillet over medium heat. Dip the bread slices in the egg mixture, then place in the skillet and cook for about 2 minutes, or until brown on one side. Turn and brown the other side. Do not overcrowd the skillet. Place the browned slices on paper towels to drain and keep warm until all the bread has been cooked.

Arrange three or four slices on each of four warm serving plates, pour the cane syrup and pecans over the bread, and sprinkle with confectioners' sugar. Serve immediately.

Pontchatoula Beignets with Bourbon Whiskey Whipped Cream

SERVES 4 TO 6

2 pints Pontchatoula
   strawberries*
1¹/₃ cups all-purpose flour
1 large egg
2 tablespoons sugar
¹/₂ teaspoon pure vanilla
   extract

6 ounces beer (not light beer)
1 quart light vegetable oil
¹/₄ cup confectioners' sugar
   Bourbon Whiskey Whipped
   Cream (see recipe below)

Carefully pick through the strawberries, removing any damaged ones. Rinse and gently dry the berries, but do not remove stems. The strawberries must be completely dry; otherwise the batter will not stick to them.

Sift the flour into a large bowl and make a well in the center. Add the egg, sugar, vanilla, and beer. Mix into a smooth batter, cover with a cloth, and let sit for 2 hours at room temperature.

In a deep-fat fryer or large deep-sided pan, heat the oil over high heat to 375 degrees on a candy thermometer. Holding the

* This is a variety of Louisiana strawberry, but any fresh strawberries may be substituted.

strawberries by the stem, dip in the batter, being careful not to bruise or break the skin. Ease the battered strawberries into the hot oil, cooking no more than six at a time. Fry for about 1 minute, or until golden brown. Remove with a slotted spoon, drain on paper towels, and keep warm until all the berries have been fried.

Dust the berries with the confectioners' sugar and serve warm. Pass the Bourbon Whiskey Whipped Cream separately.

Bourbon Whiskey Whipped Cream
MAKES 2½ CUPS

2 cups heavy cream
¼ cup Jack Daniel's whiskey
(any good-quality bourbon
may be substituted)

¼ cup confectioners' sugar

Whip the cream until it forms soft peaks. Fold in the whiskey and confectioners' sugar.

The whipped cream can be made up to 1 hour in advance and stored, covered, in the refrigerator.

Homemade Granola

SERVES 6 TO 8

1 stick (½ cup) unsalted
    butter
¾ cup honey
½ cup packed brown sugar
½ teaspoon pure vanilla
    extract
1 pound rolled oats
1½ cups shelled unsalted
    sunflower seeds

1 cup shredded coconut
    (sweetened or unsweetened,
    according to taste)
¾ cup shelled, unsalted
    pumpkin seeds
⅓ cup shelled pine nuts
½ cup shelled, unsalted
    pistachios
1½ cups slivered almonds

Preheat the oven to 325 degrees.

Combine the butter, honey, brown sugar, and vanilla in a saucepan over low heat. Cook for 5 minutes, or until the sugar has melted.

Combine all the dry ingredients in a large bowl and pour the honey mixture on top. Toss to blend thoroughly and transfer to a roasting pan.

Place in the preheated oven and bake, stirring occasionally to prevent the bottom from sticking, for about 25 minutes, or until crisp. (Baking time may vary, depending upon humidity and the oven being used.) Do not overcook; the granola will get crunchier after it is removed from the oven.

Let cool completely, then store in an airtight container until ready to serve.

Serve cold, with skim milk and sliced fresh fruit.

Fresh Berries in Champagne and Pastis

SERVES 4

½ pint fresh raspberries*
½ pint fresh blueberries*
½ pint fresh strawberries,*
stemmed
½ cup Pastis or Pernod (any
anise-flavored liqueur may
be substituted)

2 cups well-chilled champagne,
approximately

Rinse and dry the berries. Cut the strawberries into quarters. Place equal layers of fruit in four champagne glasses, beginning with a layer of raspberries, then blueberries, and finally strawberries. Cover and refrigerate for 1 hour.

Just before serving, spoon 2 tablespoons of Pastis over the fruit in each glass and fill the glasses with champagne. Serve immediately.

* Any fresh fruit, except grapes, may be substituted for the berries.

Bran Muffins

MAKES 2 DOZEN

¹/₄ cup sugar
¹/₄ cup vegetable shortening, at
    room temperature
1 teaspoon salt
2 large eggs
1 cup molasses, at room
    temperature

2 cups milk
1³/₄ cups bran
2 scant tablespoons baking
    powder
2³/₄ cups all-purpose flour,
    sifted
1 cup raisins

Preheat the oven to 400 degrees.

Cream the sugar, shortening, and salt in a large bowl. Add the eggs, one at a time, and beat well after each addition. Add the molasses, milk, bran, baking powder, and flour and mix thoroughly. Fold in the raisins.

Grease two 12-cup muffin pans, or line with paper baking cups. Fill nearly to the top and place in the preheated oven. Bake for 15 to 20 minutes, or until light brown and cooked in the center. Remove from the oven and let cool on wire racks.

Bran Muffins can be stored frozen and reheated in a warm oven.

Berry-Nut Muffins

MAKES 2 DOZEN

1 cup sugar
½ cup vegetable shortening, at room temperature
1 teaspoon salt
2 large eggs
2 cups milk
2 scant tablespoons baking powder

4 cups all-purpose flour, sifted
1½ cups fresh cranberries or blueberries*
½ cup chopped pecans or walnuts

Preheat the oven to 400 degrees.

Cream the sugar, shortening, and salt in a large bowl. Add the eggs, one at a time, and beat well after each addition. Add the milk, baking powder, and flour and mix thoroughly. Fold in the berries and nuts.

Grease two 12-cup muffin pans, or line with paper baking cups. Fill nearly to the top and place in the preheated oven. Bake for 20 to 25 minutes, or until light brown and cooked in the center. Remove from the oven and let cool on wire racks.

Berry-Nut Muffins can be stored frozen and reheated in a warm oven.

* Cranberries will make a more tart muffin than blueberries.

Currant Scones

MAKES ABOUT
3 DOZEN

¹/₂ cup black currants
4¹/₂–5 cups all-purpose flour
1 tablespoon baking
*   powder*
¹/₂ cup sugar
1¹/₂ teaspoons salt

1¹/₂ sticks (³/₄ cup) cold
*   unsalted butter, finely*
*   chopped*
1¹/₂ cups heavy cream
5 large eggs

Place the currants in a small bowl and fill with warm water to cover. Let sit for at least 15 minutes. Drain and set aside.

Using an electric mixer on low speed, combine 4 cups flour, the baking powder, ¹/₄ cup sugar, the salt, and the butter until the texture resembles a coarse meal. Add the cream and 4 eggs. Mix just until blended. The dough will be slightly sticky. Fold in the drained currants, cover with plastic wrap, and refrigerate for 1 hour.

Preheat the oven to 450 degrees.

Line a baking sheet with greased parchment or wax paper. On a lightly floured surface, knead the dough gently for 1 minute, adding flour as necessary to achieve a smooth consistency. Pat to a thickness of about ³/₄ inch. Cut into rounds with a 2-inch biscuit cutter and place on the prepared baking sheet.

Lightly beat the remaining egg and brush over the tops of the scones. Sprinkle with the remaining ¼ cup sugar.

Place in the preheated oven and bake for about 15 minutes, or until golden brown.

Serve hot with sweet butter, raspberry preserves, lemon curd, or fresh whipped cream.

XII DESSERTS

Windsor Court Strawberry Shortbread

Traditional New Orleans Pralines

Praline Brûlée

Frozen Burnt Orange Soufflé

Bourbon Whiskey Soufflé

Monkey Hill

Chocolate Breathless

Blueberry Crumble Cheesecake

Lemon Tart
with Raspberry Sauce

Pecan Squares

Cats' Tongues

Gingered Tea Sorbet

Cinnamon Ice Cream
with Raspberry Sabayon and Tulip Shells

Hazelnut Saffron Ice Cream
with Chocolate Hazelnut Sauce

Chocolate Truffles

Harlequin Mask
with Trio of Sorbets

Windsor Court Strawberry Shortbread

SERVES 8

2 pints ripe strawberries (if
   not fully ripe, sprinkle with
   sugar and let sit for about
   1 hour)
1 stick (1/2 cup) unsalted
   butter, softened
1/2 cup plus 1 tablespoon sugar

Zest and juice of 2 large
   oranges
2 teaspoons Grand Marnier
   liqueur
2 cups all-purpose flour
1 cup heavy cream

Rinse and thoroughly dry the strawberries. Stem and slice 1
pint. Purée the remaining berries in a food processor fitted
with the metal blade. Strain to remove the seeds. Set aside.

In a large bowl, cream the butter with 1/4 cup sugar, the
orange zest and juice, and 1 teaspoon Grand Marnier. Blend 3/4
cup flour into the creamed mixture. Lightly stir in the remaining 1 1/4 cups flour, being careful not to overwork the dough.
Gather into a smooth ball, wrap in a damp cloth, and refrigerate for at least 1 hour, or overnight.

Preheat the oven to 400 degrees. Place eight serving plates in
the freezer to chill.

Divide the dough in half. Return one portion to the refrigerator and roll out the other portion on a lightly floured surface to
a thickness of about 1/4 inch. Using a 4-inch cookie cutter, cut
into hearts or circles. Repeat with the remaining dough. You

should have 16 hearts or circles. Place on ungreased cookie sheets and bake in the preheated oven for 10 to 15 minutes, or until golden brown. Place on wire racks to cool.

Combine ¼ cup sugar and 1 tablespoon water in a heavy saucepan over medium-high heat. Cook for 3 minutes, or until the sugar melts and turns light brown. Dip the top surface of 8 shortbread hearts or circles into the caramelized sugar and set on wax paper, caramelized side up, for 5 minutes, or until the caramel sets.

Whip the cream with the remaining tablespoon sugar until it forms stiff peaks. Stir in the remaining teaspoon Grand Marnier.

Place one uncoated shortbread heart on each of eight chilled serving plates. Spoon on some whipped cream, then top with a layer of strawberry halves. Spoon on additional cream and top with a caramel-coated heart. Spoon the puréed strawberries around the shortbread and serve immediately.

Traditional New Orleans Pralines

MAKES
APPROXIMATELY
5 DOZEN

1 stick (¹/₂ cup) unsalted butter
1 cup heavy cream
2 cups granulated sugar

2¹/₄ cups packed brown sugar
1 pound pecan pieces,
  chopped

Spread sheets of wax paper over two baking sheets.

In a heavy saucepan over high heat, combine the butter, cream, and sugars and bring to a boil. Stir in the pecans. When the mixture returns to a boil, remove from the heat.

Drop the praline mixture from a soup spoon to make 1¹/₂-inch circles on the wax paper. The mixture will crystallize rapidly, so work quickly. Let harden at room temperature for 6 hours.

The pralines may be stored in airtight containers for up to 2 weeks.

Praline Brûlée

SERVES 4

3 cups heavy cream
8 large egg yolks
½ cup plus 2 tablespoons sugar
½ cup hazelnut paste (available
   in specialty food stores and
   some supermarkets)

4 Traditional New Orleans
  Pralines (see page 215)

Heat the cream for about 2 minutes, until hot but not boiling, in a heavy saucepan over medium-high heat. Remove from the heat. In the top half of a double boiler, combine the yolks, ½ cup sugar, and the hazelnut paste. Place over simmering water and whisk for about 4 minutes, or until creamy and thick. Add the hot cream and cook, stirring constantly, until the mixture is thick enough to form ribbons when the whisk is pulled through. Remove from the heat and immediately place in the refrigerator. Chill for at least 8 hours.

Preheat the broiler.

Just before serving, spoon the well-chilled mixture into four individual ramekins or custard cups. Sprinkle the remaining 2 tablespoons sugar on top and place under the preheated broiler to caramelize and brown the sugar. Keep the oven door open and watch carefully to prevent scorching.

Serve immediately, garnished with a praline on top of each brûlée.

Frozen Burnt Orange Soufflé

SERVES 4

*¹/₄ cup granulated sugar
Juice and grated zest of 4
  oranges
2 tablespoons orange
  marmalade
1¹/₂ cups heavy cream
4 large egg yolks*

*2 tablespoons Grand Marnier
  liqueur
1 tablespoon confectioners'
  sugar
8 orange segments
4 fresh mint leaves*

Fit the outside of four ³/₄-cup soufflé molds or ramekins with a parchment paper or aluminum collar to stand about an inch above the rim of the mold. Secure with tape and set aside.

In a heavy saucepan, combine the granulated sugar and 1 tablespoon water. Place over medium-high heat and cook until the sugar melts and the liquid turns golden brown. Stir in the orange juice, zest, and marmalade. Bring the mixture back to a boil and cook until it forms a soft ball (234 degrees on a candy thermometer).

While the sugar-orange mixture is cooking, whip the cream until it forms stiff peaks. Set aside.

Place the egg yolks in the bowl of an electric mixer. Beating constantly on medium speed, add the cooked sugar mixture to the eggs in a slow, steady stream. When all the syrup has been added, increase the speed to high and beat until completely cool, scraping the sides of the bowl frequently.

Stir in the Grand Marnier. Lightly stir about a quarter of the whipped cream into the egg mixture, then carefully fold in the remaining whipped cream.

Fill the soufflé molds to just below the rim of the paper or foil band and freeze for at least 8 hours.

To serve, remove the collars but do not unmold. Place one soufflé mold on each of four dessert plates and sprinkle with confectioners' sugar. Garnish each plate with orange segments and a mint leaf and serve immediately.

Bourbon Whiskey Soufflé

SERVES 8

1 stick (¹/₂ cup) plus 2
    tablespoons unsalted butter
1 cup plus 2 tablespoons
    granulated sugar
³/₄ cup raisins
³/₄ cup bourbon

2 cups milk
1 cup sifted all-purpose flour
8 large eggs, separated
1 tablespoon confectioners'
    sugar

Using 2 tablespoons butter, generously butter one 1-quart or eight ¹/₂-cup soufflé molds. Coat the insides of the molds with 2 tablespoons granulated sugar. Set aside.

Combine the raisins and bourbon in a small bowl. Let sit at room temperature for 2 hours.

Place the milk and remaining stick butter in a heavy sauce-pan over medium heat and bring to a boil. Lower the heat and gradually stir in the flour to make a thick paste. Beat briskly with a wooden spoon until the mixture pulls cleanly away from the side of the pan. Remove from the heat and transfer to a large bowl to cool.

Preheat the oven to 375 degrees.

Stir the 8 egg yolks into the flour mixture with a wooden spoon, then add the bourbon and raisins.

Whip the 8 egg whites until stiff, then add the remaining cup granulated sugar and beat to a glossy meringue. Stir about a quarter of the meringue into the raisin mixture, then gently fold in the remaining meringue, rotating the bowl and cutting through the mixture.

Pour the batter into the prepared molds and wipe any drips from the sides. Place in the preheated oven and bake for 35 minutes, or until a thin crust has formed on top. Remove from the oven, sprinkle with confectioners' sugar, and serve immediately.

Monkey Hill

SERVES 4

2 ounces semisweet chocolate, grated

2 Traditional New Orleans Pralines, crumbled (see page 215)

2 ounces candied chestnuts (available at specialty food stores), diced

4 large egg yolks

1/4 cup confectioners' sugar

1 teaspoon pure vanilla extract

1 cup heavy cream

1/2 stick (1/4 cup) butter, softened

5 ounces white chocolate, melted

2 ounces semisweet chocolate, melted

In a small bowl, combine the grated semisweet chocolate, pralines, and candied chestnuts and stir to blend. Divide among four martini or saucer-shaped champagne glasses and place in the refrigerator to chill.

In a medium bowl, beat the yolks and confectioners' sugar together until the mixture is thick and pale yellow. Stir in the vanilla and set aside.

Whip the cream until it forms stiff peaks. In a large bowl, combine the butter and white chocolate. Fold the yolk mixture into the chocolate, then gently fold in the whipped cream, a third at a time.

Chill the mousse for about 2 hours, or until firm, then spoon into the glasses, over the praline mixture. Drizzle the melted semisweet chocolate over the mousse and serve immediately.

Chocolate Breathless

MAKES 12

1 pound semisweet chocolate,
  broken into pieces
4 large eggs, separated
⅓ cup dark rum
3 cups heavy cream
⅓ cup plus ¾ cup granulated
  sugar

7 large egg whites
1 heaping cup plus 2
  tablespoons confectioners'
  sugar
¾ cup unsweetened cocoa
  powder

Place the chocolate in the top half of a double boiler over simmering water to melt. Place the egg yolks in a large bowl, add ⅓ cup water and the rum and whisk to blend thoroughly. Stir in the melted chocolate.

Whip the cream until it forms stiff peaks.

In a medium bowl, beat 4 egg whites until foamy. Add ⅓ cup granulated sugar and continue to beat until the mixture forms stiff peaks. Fold the beaten egg whites into the chocolate mixture, then fold in the whipped cream. Refrigerate until ready to serve.

Preheat the oven to 150 degrees.

In a large bowl, beat 7 egg whites until foamy. Add the remaining ¾ cup granulated sugar and continue to beat until the mixture forms stiff peaks. Sift together 1 heaping cup of confectioners' sugar and the cocoa, then fold gently into the meringue. Do not overmix. Spoon the mixture into a pastry bag fitted with a plain ½-inch tube.

Line two baking sheets with parchment or wax paper. Pipe thirty-six 2-inch disks onto the sheet, about an inch apart. Pipe long lines with the rest of the meringue. Place in the preheated oven, with the oven door left open 1 inch, and bake for about 1½ hours or until firm. Remove from the oven and let cool.

The chocolate meringue can be made 1 day in advance and stored in a dry, airtight container until ready to serve.

Chop the meringue lines into ½-inch pieces and set aside. Place a meringue disk on a flat work surface and top with a layer of chocolate mousse. Add another meringue disk, then more mousse. Complete the stack with another layer of meringue. Frost the top and sides of the stack with mousse, then sprinkle chopped meringue pieces on top. Repeat the assembly with the remaining meringue disks, making twelve servings in all.

Place one Breathless on each of twelve serving plates and dust the tops lightly with the remaining 2 tablespoons confectioners' sugar. Serve immediately.

Blueberry Crumble Cheesecake

MAKES ONE
10-INCH CAKE

2¹/₂ sticks (1¹/₄ cups) unsalted
    butter, chilled
1 cup plus 2 tablespoons
    sugar
³/₄ teaspoon pure vanilla
    extract
    Salt
1¹/₄ cups plus 1 tablespoon all-
    purpose flour

14 ounces cream cheese,
    softened
    Freshly squeezed juice of
¹/₂ lemon
8 large egg yolks
    Pinch of baking powder
¹/₄ cup apricot preserves
1 pint blueberries, rinsed and
    dried

Remove ¹/₂ stick butter from the refrigerator and let sit at room temperature until soft.

In a large bowl, cream together the butter, 2 tablespoons sugar, ¹/₄ teaspoon vanilla, and a pinch of salt. When well blended, work in ³/₄ cup flour. If more liquid is needed to make a smooth dough, gradually add 2 to 3 teaspoons ice water. Form into a ball, wrap in plastic wrap, and refrigerate for 20 minutes.

Preheat the oven to 350 degrees.

On a lightly floured surface, roll out the dough with a rolling pin until it is about ¹/₄ inch thick. Center a 10-inch springform pan on the dough and trim around the edge to make a circle of dough. Transfer to an ungreased baking sheet and prick with a fork. Place in the preheated oven and bake for 10 minutes. Remove from the oven and set aside to cool. Leave the oven at 350 degrees.

Melt 1½ sticks butter in a small saucepan over low heat. In a large bowl, beat together the cream cheese and ¾ cup sugar. When well blended, add the lemon juice, a pinch of salt, and the remaining ½ teaspoon vanilla. Stir in 1 tablespoon flour, then add the egg yolks one at a time, stirring after each addition. Beating constantly with an electric mixer set on low speed, add the melted butter in a slow, steady stream. Set aside.

Using a pastry blender, combine the remaining ½ stick butter and ¼ cup sugar in a medium bowl. Cut in the remaining ½ cup flour and the baking powder to form pea-size crumbs. Do not overmix.

To assemble, place the baked crust in the bottom of the springform pan. Spread the apricot preserves over the crust. Add the blueberries in a layer, followed by the cream cheese filling. Sprinkle the crumble on top and place in the preheated oven. Bake for about 30 minutes, or until the crumble is golden brown. Remove from the oven and set aside to cool.

The cheesecake may be served at room temperature or stored, uncovered, in the refrigerator and served chilled.

Lemon Tart with Raspberry Sauce

**MAKES AN
11-INCH TART**

1¼ cups all-purpose flour
½ teaspoon salt
1¼ cups plus 2 teaspoons sugar
½ cup vegetable shortening
¼ cup milk, approximately
5 large whole eggs
5 large egg yolks

Freshly squeezed juice of
5 lemons
Grated zest of 2 lemons
6 tablespoons Clarified Butter
(see page 180)
Raspberry Sauce (see recipe
below)

Sift the flour with the salt and 2 teaspoons sugar into a large bowl. Cut the shortening into the mixture with a fork or pastry blender until the texture resembles a coarse meal. Make a well in the center and pour in about ¼ cup milk. Quickly mix in the milk and check the consistency. If the dough is tight, add additional milk, a tablespoon at a time, until the dough is moist but not sticky. Gather into a ball, cover with plastic wrap, and refrigerate for 30 minutes.

Turn the dough out onto a lightly floured work surface and roll into a circle about 13 inches in diameter. Carefully wrap the dough around the rolling pin and unroll it over an 11-inch tart pan. Press into the bottom and sides of the pan and roll the pin across the top to cut off the excess dough. Prick the bottom of the crust with a fork and refrigerate for 15 minutes.

Preheat the oven to 375 degrees.

Just before baking, line the chilled crust with parchment or foil and partially fill with pastry weights, dried beans, or rice to weight the dough. Place in the preheated oven and bake for 20 minutes, or until the edges are lightly browned. Remove the beans and liner and return the pastry shell to the oven for about 5 minutes, or until the center of the crust is brown. Remove from the oven and place on a wire rack to cool.

In the top half of a double boiler over simmering water, combine the whole eggs, yolks, remaining 1¼ cups sugar, lemon juice, and zest. Whisk rapidly for about 10 minutes, or until the filling thickens and forms ridges when the whisk is drawn through.

Preheat the broiler.

Remove the lemon filling from the heat and whisk in the butter. Pour into the baked crust and smooth the top. Place under the broiler for 1 minute, or until the top is lightly browned. Remove from the broiler and refrigerate until ready to serve.

Cut into slices and place on individual dessert plates. Spoon Raspberry Sauce over the pie and serve immediately.

Raspberry Sauce
MAKES 2 CUPS

2 pints fresh raspberries, rinsed and dried
2 tablespoons honey

2 teaspoons sugar (or to taste)
Freshly squeezed juice of ½ lime

Push the berries through a fine sieve into a bowl. Discard the seeds and pulp remaining in the sieve. Combine the berry purée with the remaining ingredients and mix well.

This may be made a day or two in advance and stored, covered, in the refrigerator. Serve either cold or at room temperature.

Pecan Squares

MAKES 6 DOZEN

4 sticks (1 pound) unsalted
   butter, softened
1 cup confectioners' sugar
1 large egg yolk
2 drops pure lemon extract
   Dash of salt
2³/₄ cups sifted cake flour

¹/₂ cup honey
¹/₄ cup granulated sugar
1 cup firmly packed brown
   sugar
2¹/₂ cups pecan pieces
¹/₄ cup heavy cream

In a large bowl, cream 2 sticks butter, the confectioners' sugar, egg yolk, lemon extract, and salt using an electric mixer on low speed, until light and fluffy. Keeping the mixer on low speed, add the flour, in thirds, being careful not to overwork the dough. Gather into a smooth ball, wrap in plastic wrap, and chill for 1 hour.

Preheat the oven to 350 degrees.

Using your hands or a rolling pin, on a lightly floured work surface flatten the dough into a rough sheet about ¹/₈ inch thick. Transfer to a 15¹/₂- by 10¹/₂-inch jellyroll pan and press into the bottom and sides of the pan. Prick the bottom of the crust with a fork and place in the preheated oven. Bake for about 20 minutes, or until the crust is tacky to the touch.

Remove from the oven and set aside. Leave the oven at 350 degrees.

Combine the remaining 2 sticks butter, and the honey and granulated and brown sugars in a deep saucepan over high heat and bring to a boil. Cook for 3 minutes. Remove from the heat and stir in the pecans and cream. Immediately spread the hot mixture evenly over the sugar dough. Place in the preheated oven and bake for 20 minutes, or until set.

Let cool partially, then cut into 1½-inch squares. Pecan Squares can be stored, covered, at room temperature for up to 1 week.

Cats' Tongues

MAKES
APPROXIMATELY
3½ DOZEN

2 sticks (1 cup) unsalted
  butter, softened
2½ cups sifted confectioners'
  sugar
5 large egg whites
3 cups sifted all-purpose flour

3 drops pure lemon extract
½ cup raspberry jam,
  approximately
8 ounces semisweet chocolate,
  melted

Preheat the oven to 400 degrees.

Using an electric mixer, cream the butter with the sugar. At low speed, add the egg whites and mix just to partially blend. The mixture should still be lumpy. Fold in the flour and lemon extract. Do not overmix. Fit a pastry bag with a ½- or ¾-inch plain tube and fill with the dough.

Line a baking sheet with parchment or wax paper. Pipe even lines of batter 2 inches long and 1 inch apart onto the baking sheet. Place in the preheated oven and bake for 10 to 12 minutes, or until lightly browned around the edges. Place on wire racks to cool.

Spread a thin layer of raspberry jam on half the wafers and top each with another wafer. Holding each cookie sandwich by one end, dip halfway into the melted chocolate. Set on wax paper and refrigerate until the chocolate hardens.

These cookies may be stored in an airtight container at room temperature for up to 2 days. Cover and refrigerate for longer storage.

Gingered Tea Sorbet

MAKES 1 QUART

4 cups freshly brewed tea
2 ounces fresh gingerroot,
  peeled and chopped

1 cup light corn syrup

Combine the ingredients in a heavy stock pot over high heat and bring to a boil. Cook for 2 minutes, then remove from the heat and let sit for 1 hour.

Strain the mixture into an ice cream freezer and freeze according to the manufacturer's instructions. (Or strain into a wide, shallow dish and place in the freezer. Stir every 10 minutes until smooth and stiff. The more the sorbet is stirred, the finer the ice crystals.)

Serve alone as an intermezzo or light dessert, or spooned onto a fresh fruit salad.

Cinnamon Ice Cream with Raspberry Sabayon and Tulip Shells

SERVES 10

2 cups heavy cream
2 cups milk
³/₄ cup granulated sugar
3 cinnamon sticks
10 large egg yolks
   Raspberry Sabayon (see recipe below)

Tulip Shells (see recipe below)
1 pint raspberries, rinsed and dried
¹/₄ cup confectioners' sugar
10 large fresh mint leaves

Combine the cream, milk, granulated sugar, and cinnamon sticks in a heavy saucepan over medium heat and bring to a boil. As soon as the mixture boils, remove from the heat and discard the cinnamon sticks. Place the egg yolks in a large bowl and whisk to blend. Add the hot milk mixture to the yolks, a little at a time, whisking constantly.

When all the milk mixture has been incorporated, strain into a clean, heavy saucepan and place over medium-low heat. Cook, stirring constantly with a wooden spoon, for about 10 minutes, or until the mixture is thick enough to coat the back of the spoon. Remove from the heat and let cool to room temperature.

Pour into an ice cream maker and freeze according to the manufacturer's instructions. (Or pour into a large shallow bowl and place in the freezer. Stir every 10 to 15 minutes until the ice cream has set.) While the ice cream is freezing, place ten serving plates in the freezer to chill.

When ready to serve, spoon a circle of Raspberry Sabayon onto each of the chilled plates. Place a Tulip Shell in the center. Fill the shells with Cinnamon Ice Cream and sprinkle a few raspberries on top. Dust with confectioners' sugar, garnish with a mint leaf, and serve immediately.

Raspberry Sabayon
MAKES 2 CUPS

5 large egg yolks
1/2 cup sugar
1/4 cup champagne

2 tablespoons framboise
  (raspberry liqueur)
1 1/4 cups heavy cream

In the top half of a double boiler over simmering water, combine the egg yolks, sugar, champagne, and framboise. Cook, whisking constantly, for 10 minutes, or until the mixture thickens. Transfer to a large bowl and whisk until cool.

Whip the cream until it forms firm peaks. Gently fold into the egg yolk mixture.

Raspberry Sabayon may be made up to 2 days ahead and stored, covered, in the refrigerator until ready to serve.

Tulip Shells
MAKES 10 SHELLS

1/2 cup plus 2 tablespoons all-
  purpose flour
1 cup confectioners' sugar
1/2 stick (1/4 cup) unsalted
  butter, melted

3 tablespoons heavy cream
1/2 teaspoon pure vanilla extract
3 large egg whites
  Pinch of salt

Preheat the oven to 400 degrees. Invert eight custard cups on a flat work surface near the oven.

Sift the flour and sugar together into a large bowl. Gradually stir in the melted butter. Add the cream, vanilla, egg whites, and salt and stir to blend.

Grease a baking sheet with vegetable shortening or vegetable oil. Using a tablespoon, drop the batter onto the baking sheet and spread, with the back of the spoon, to form a 5-inch circle. The dough will spread farther as it bakes, so make only three or four shells at a time.

Place in the preheated oven and bake for 15 minutes, or just until the edges are brown. Watch closely to avoid overbaking. Remove from the oven and carefully lift each cookie with a spatula onto an inverted custard cup. Place another cup on top, working quickly while the cookies are still hot and pliable. As soon as the cookies are cool, remove the custard cups and prepare another batch of batter for baking.

The cooled cookie shells are very fragile, so handle gently. Store in a large airtight container until ready to serve.

Hazelnut Saffron Ice Cream with Chocolate Hazelnut Sauce

2 tablespoons unsalted butter
1/2 teaspoon saffron
2 cups milk
1 cup sugar
10 large egg yolks
2 cups heavy cream

1/2 cup roasted hazelnuts,
  crushed (roasted pistachios
  may be substituted)
Chocolate Hazelnut Sauce
(see recipe below)

Place the butter in a medium saucepan and set over low heat to melt. Remove from the heat. Add the saffron and steep for 5 to 10 minutes, or until the color of the saffron deepens and intensifies. Add the milk and sugar. Place over medium heat and bring to a boil. Remove from the heat and set aside.

In a large bowl, beat the egg yolks until just blended. Whisk in the cream, then strain into a clean bowl. Gradually whisk in the hot milk mixture, stirring vigorously. Stir in the crushed nuts.

Pour into an ice cream maker and freeze according to the manufacturer's instructions. (Or pour into a wide, shallow dish and place in the freezer. When partially frozen, transfer to a bowl and beat until smooth. Pour back into the dish and return to the freezer. Repeat the process, beating once or twice more, until stiff.)

Spoon equal portions into individual dessert dishes and pour Chocolate Hazelnut Sauce over the ice cream. Serve immediately.

Chocolate Hazelnut Sauce

MAKES 1½ CUPS

1 cup heavy cream
¼ cup sugar
4 ounces semisweet chocolate, chopped

1 tablespoon hazelnut liqueur (Frangelica or B & B)

Place the cream and sugar in a small heavy saucepan over high heat and bring to a boil. Remove from the heat and add the chocolate. Stir until the chocolate has melted, then add the liqueur. Serve at room temperature.

Chocolate Hazelnut Sauce can be stored, covered, in the refrigerator (do not freeze) for up to 1 week.

Chocolate Truffles

MAKES ABOUT
4 DOZEN

2 sticks (1 cup) unsalted
  butter
2 cups heavy cream
1/2 cup Chambord liqueur
28 ounces semisweet chocolate,
  chopped

1/2 cup unsweetened cocoa
  powder
1/2 cup confectioners' sugar

Place the butter, cream, and Chambord in the top half of a double boiler over simmering water and heat until almost boiling. Remove from the heat and gradually fold in the chopped chocolate. Stir until the chocolate is melted and the mixture is smooth and glossy. Transfer to a bowl and let cool to room temperature. Refrigerate for about 24 hours, or until very firm.

Shape the mixture into balls using a teaspoon or melon baller. Chill until firm.

Blend the cocoa and confectioners' sugar in a shallow dish. Roll the truffles in the cocoa mixture until completely coated.

The truffles may be stored in an airtight container in the refrigerator for up to 2 weeks.

Harlequin Mask with Trio of Sorbets

SERVES 12

¹/₂ *cup all-purpose flour*
¹/₂ *cup confectioners' sugar*
   Pinch of cinnamon
¹/₂ *teaspoon pure vanilla extract*
 4 *egg whites*
   Heavy cream, if needed
 1 *teaspoon unsweetened cocoa powder*

Vegetable oil spray
Raspberry Sorbet (see recipe below)
Passion Fruit Sorbet (see recipe below)
Melon Sorbet (see recipe below)

Trace a mask shape, about 7 inches long, onto a piece of cardboard, making sure that you allow a border. Cut the shape out, leaving a mask stencil with straight edges and a 2-inch border all around. Cut around the eyes, leaving them attached to the upper edge of the stencil by a thin strip of cardboard.*

Sift the flour and confectioners' sugar together into a large bowl. With an electric mixer on low speed, add the cinnamon and vanilla, then the egg whites, one by one, mixing well to make a paste. Let the mixture sit in the bowl for 45 minutes at

* In addition to the traditional Harlequin mask, animal faces or any simple mask shape will work with this recipe.

room temperature. (If the paste is still thick after 45 minutes, thin with a small amount of heavy cream.)

Mix 2 tablespoons of the paste with the cocoa and place in a pastry bag with a narrow tip. Set aside.

Preheat the oven to 375 degrees.

Cover a baking sheet with parchment paper and spray lightly with vegetable oil spray. Lay the mask stencil on top of the greased paper. Using a spatula, spread a thin layer of paste over the mask. Lift up the stencil and repeat to make twelve masks in all.

Using the pastry bag, pipe a thin band of chocolate paste ½ inch wide along the edge of each mask. Draw a toothpick through the chocolate band using an up-and-down motion to create a decorative effect resembling feathers. (See photo section.) Place in the preheated oven and bake for 10 minutes, or until the dough begins to turn golden.

Remove from the oven and immediately peel each mask, one at a time, off the paper. Place a large round canister on its side and wrap the masks around the canister to give them a curved shape. Let cool on the canister before handling. The masks can be stored in an airtight container for up to 8 hours.

Prop each mask against a tall champagne or martini glass filled with one scoop each of Raspberry, Passion Fruit, and Melon Sorbets. Serve immediately.

Raspberry Sorbet
MAKES 2 CUPS

1 pound raspberries, rinsed and
   dried
1 cup sugar

Freshly squeezed juice of
   ½ lemon

Purée the raspberries in a blender or food processor fitted with the metal blade. Transfer to a fine strainer positioned over a bowl. Reserve the purée and the liquid that collects in the bowl.

Combine the sugar and 2 cups water in a heavy stock pot over high heat and bring to a boil. Cook for 2 minutes, then remove from the heat and let sit for 1 hour, or until cooled to room temperature.

Add the raspberry purée and liquid and the lemon juice to the sugar and mix well. Strain into an ice cream freezer and freeze according to the manufacturer's instructions. (Or strain into a wide, shallow dish and place in the freezer. Stir every 10 minutes until smooth and stiff. The more the sorbet is stirred, the finer the ice crystals.)

Passion Fruit Sorbet
MAKES 2 CUPS

20 passion fruit   1 cup sugar

Cut the passion fruit in half. Spoon out the seeds and pulp and purée in a blender or food processor fitted with the metal blade. Transfer to a fine strainer positioned over a bowl. Reserve the purée and the liquid that collects in the bowl.

Combine the sugar and 2 cups water in a heavy stock pot over high heat and bring to a boil. Cook for 2 minutes, then remove from the heat and let sit for 1 hour, or until cooled to room temperature.

Add the passion fruit purée and liquid to the sugar and mix well. Strain into an ice cream freezer and freeze according to the manufacturer's instructions. (Or strain into a wide, shallow dish and place in the freezer. Stir every 10 minutes until smooth and stiff. The more the sorbet is stirred, the finer the ice crystals.)

Melon Sorbet
MAKES 2 CUPS

1 one-and-a-half-pound   1 cup sugar
   honeydew melon   1 teaspoon honey

Cut the melon in half, and remove and discard the seeds. Scoop out the melon pulp and purée in a blender or food processor fitted with the metal blade. Transfer to a fine strainer positioned over a bowl. Reserve the purée and the liquid that collects in the bowl.

Combine the sugar and 2 cups water in a heavy stock pot over high heat and bring to a boil. Cook for 2 minutes, then remove from the heat and let sit for 1 hour, or until cooled to room temperature.

Add the melon purée and liquid and the honey to the sugar and mix well. Strain into an ice cream freezer and freeze according to the manufacturer's instructions. (Or strain into a wide, shallow dish and place in the freezer. Stir every 10 minutes until smooth and stiff. The more the sorbet is stirred, the finer the ice crystals.)

INDEX

A

almonds, sugared toasted,
  shredded spinach salad with
  creamy vinaigrette and, 22–23
appetizers:
  beggar's purses with caviar,
    57–58
  confit of duck legs and lentils,
    64–65
  crabmeat soufflé, 44–45
  crawfish Sarah Jane, 33
  crawfish sausage, 34–36
  fried frog's legs with champagne
    mustard sauce, 55–56
  grilled foie gras and pears, 59–60
  oysters polo, 38–39
  pâté of salmon and crabmeat en
    croûte, 46–48
  potted crawfish, 37
  quenelles of seafood with
    tarragon cream sauce, 49–50
  rillettes of lobster and avocado
    with cilantro yogurt sauce,
    42–43
  sautéed snails with Folsom
    chanterelles, 53–54
  shrimp sautéed with citrus fruit,
    40–41
  smoked redfish with cucumber
    jam, 51–52
  steak Romanoff, 66
  terrine of chicken and goose
    livers with Cumberland sauce,
    61–63

apple raisin chutney, grilled tea-
  marinated duck breasts
  with duck cracklings and,
  111–112
artichoke-oyster soup, 5
artichokes, baby, linguine with feta,
  pancetta, and, 79–80
avocado, rillettes of lobster and,
  with cilantro yogurt sauce,
  42–43

B

basil:
  crabmeat sauce, shrimp spaetzle
    with, 74–75
  fresh herb cheese with endive
    and Bibb lettuce, 28–29
  gazpacho with cumin, crabmeat,
    and, 13–14
  pesto, chiffonade of lamb with,
    141–142
bean(s):
  black, salsa, grilled marinated
    scallops with, 102–103
  J. D.'s duck chili, 113–114
  white, cassoulet with chicken
    and, 121–122
béarnaise sauce, tomato, 194
béchamel sauce, 175
beef:
  demi-glace, 171–172
  roast tenderloin of, with Creole
    cardinal sauce, 147–148
  steak Romanoff, 66

beef (*continued*)
   tournedos of, with red butter and
      beef marrow, 149–150
beggar's purses with caviar, 57–58
beignets, Pontchatoula, with
      bourbon whiskey whipped
      cream, 201–202
berry(ies):
   blueberry crumble cheesecake,
      226–227
   fresh, in champagne and Pastis,
      205
   nut muffins, 207
   see also raspberry(ies);
      strawberry(ies)
beurre blanc:
   cayenne, 35
   #1, 173
   #2, 174
   wasabi, tuna with two sesames,
      shiitake mushrooms, and,
      94–95
blueberry(ies):
   crumble cheesecake, 226–227
   fresh berries in champagne and
      Pastis, 205
   nut muffins, 207
bordelaise sauce, cumin coriander,
      grilled rack of lamb with,
      139–140
bourbon whiskey:
   soufflé, 220–221
   whipped cream, Pontchatoula
      beignets with, 201–202
bran muffins, 206
breakfast and brunch:
   berry-nut muffins, 207
   bran muffins, 206
   currant scones, 208–209
   eggs Windsor Court, 193–194
   fresh berries in champagne and
      Pastis, 205

homemade granola, 203–204
   omelette Linley, 197–198
   pain Perdu, 199–200
   Pontchatoula beignets with
      bourbon whiskey whipped
      cream, 201–202
   scrambled eggs with peppered
      lobster, 195–196
brûlée, praline, 216–217
butter:
   clarified, 180
   potted crawfish, 37
   red, tournedos of beef with beef
      marrow and, 149–150
   spiced glazing, 182
   Tabasco-mint compound, 184
   see also beurre blanc

C

caper-tomato relish, 186
caponata relish, Billy's mother's,
      grilled veal chops with,
      143–144
cashew-breaded duck breasts with
      peanut sauce, 115–116
cats' tongues, 232–233
caviar:
   beggar's purses with, 57–58
   eggs Windsor Court, 193–194
cayenne beurre blanc, 35
celery and pink peppercorn
      dressing, lamb's lettuce salad
      with, 21
champagne:
   fresh berries in Pastis and, 205
   mustard sauce, fried frog's legs
      with, 55–56
   strawberry soup, 10
cheese:
   basil pesto, 142

feta, linguine with pancetta, baby artichokes, and, 79–80

fresh herb, with endive and Bibb lettuce, 28–29

see also Parmesan

cheesecake, blueberry crumble, 226–227

chicken:

breasts, grilled, with vinegar-seared raspberries, 117–118

cassoulet with white beans and, 121–122

demi-glace, 171–172

grilled satay of, with ginger sauce, 119–120

livers, terrine of goose livers and, with Cumberland sauce, 61–63

stock, 169

chili, J. D.'s duck, 113–114

chocolate:

breathless, 224–225

cats' tongues, 232–233

hazelnut sauce, hazelnut saffron ice cream with, 238–239

monkey hill, 222–223

truffles, 240

chutney, apple raisin, 112

cilantro:

and shrimp bisque, 3–4

and turmeric pilaf, 163

yogurt sauce, rillettes of lobster and avocado with, 42–43

cinnamon ice cream with raspberry sabayon and tulip shells, 235–237

citrus (fruit):

mayonnaise, lobster poached in honeyed water with, 98–99

shrimp sautéed with, 40–41

see also lemon; orange coffee

mandarin glaze, Chinese lacquered duck with, 109–110

coriander:

cumin bordelaise sauce, grilled rack of lamb with, 139–140

port sauce, roasted Abita Springs quail with, 127–128

corn and crab soup with corn fritters, 6–7

crab(meat):

basil sauce, shrimp spaetzle with, 74–75

cakes, Louisiana, with fresh tomato tartar sauce, 96–97

and corn soup with corn fritters, 6–7

dressing, hot, spinach salad with, 19

gazpacho with cumin, basil, and, 13–14

pâté of salmon and, en croûte, 46–48

roulade of veal with spinach, pine nuts, and, and Marsala sauce, 145–146

soufflé, 44–45

cranberry-nut muffins, 207

crawfish:

hot, with gingered sesame on watercress, 25–26

potted, 37

Sarah Jane, 33

sausage, 34–36

and shrimp stuffing, sugarcane pasta with, 72–73

cucumber:

jam, smoked redfish with, 51–52

salad, 24

cumin:

coriander bordelaise sauce, grilled rack of lamb with, 139–140

cumin (*continued*)
    gazpacho with basil, crabmeat, and, 13–14
currant scones, 208–209
curry powder, Harvey's, 188

D

demi-glace, 171–172
desserts:
    blueberry crumble cheesecake, 226–227
    bourbon whiskey soufflé, 220–221
    cats' tongues, 232–233
    chocolate breathless, 224–225
    chocolate truffles, 240
    cinnamon ice cream with raspberry sabayon and tulip shells, 235–237
    frozen burnt orange soufflé, 218–219
    gingered tea sorbet, 234
    Harlequin mask with trio of sorbets, 241–244
    hazelnut saffron ice cream with chocolate hazelnut sauce, 238–239
    lemon tart with raspberry sauce, 228–229
    monkey hill, 222–223
    pecan squares, 230–231
    praline brûlée, 216–217
    traditional New Orleans pralines, 215
    Windsor Court strawberry shortbread, 213–214
duck:
    breasts, cashew-breaded, with peanut sauce, 115–116
    breasts, grilled tea-marinated, with duck cracklings and apple raisin chutney, 111–112
    chili, J. D.'s, 113–114
    Chinese lacquered, with coffee mandarin glaze, 109–110
    grilled foie gras and pears, 59–60
    legs, confit of, and lentils, 64–65
    wild, braised with port, 131–132
    ziti with lobster, cream, and, 70–71

E

egg(s):
    omelette Linley, 197–198
    scrambled, with peppered lobster, 195–196
    wash, 190
    Windsor Court, 193–194
eggplant:
    Billy's mother's caponata relish, 144
    Creole ratatouille, 160
    stuffed squash blossoms, 161–162
endive, fresh herb cheese with Bibb lettuce and, 28–29

F

feta, linguine with pancetta, baby artichokes, and, 79–80
fish:
    harlequin of three, with sun-dried tomato sauce, 104–106
    mousse, 93
    quenelles of seafood with tarragon cream sauce, 49–50
    red snapper with vanilla, 88–89
    smoked redfish with cucumber jam, 51–52
    sole fillets with lavender, 100–101

stock, 170
tuna with two sesames, wasabi
beurre blanc, and shiitake
mushrooms, 94–95
see also grouper; salmon; shellfish
foie gras, grilled pears and,
59–60
fowl:
pheasant and juniper ravioli with
wild morel sauce, 76–78
stuffed turkey breast with roast
gravy, 123–124
terrine of chicken and goose
livers with Cumberland sauce,
61–63
see also chicken; duck
fritters, corn, crab and corn soup
with, 6–7
frog's legs, fried, with champagne
mustard sauce, 55–56

G

game:
medallions of venison with
chanterelles, 133–134
panéed loin of rabbit thermidor,
129–130
roasted Abita Springs quail with
port-coriander sauce, 127–128
wild fowl braised with port,
131–132
garlic spread, 183
gazpacho with cumin, basil, and
crabmeat, 13–14
gingered:
sesame, hot crawfish with, on
watercress, 25–26
tea sorbet, 234
ginger sauce, grilled satay of
chicken with, 119–120
goose livers, terrine of chicken

livers and, with Cumberland
sauce, 61–63
granola, homemade, 203–204
grouper:
fish stock, 170
grilled, with frozen Pernod
vinaigrette, 90–91
harlequin of three fish with sun-
dried tomato sauce, 104–106
Napoleon of, 92–93
quenelles of seafood with
tarragon cream sauce, 49–50
rosette of salmon and, with
green peppercorn sauce, 84–85

H

Harlequin mask with trio of
sorbets, 241–244
harlequin of three fish with sun-
dried tomato sauce, 104–106
hazelnut:
chocolate sauce, 239
praline brûlée, 216–217
saffron ice cream with chocolate
hazelnut sauce, 238–239
hollandaise sauce, 176–177
honeyed water, lobster poached in,
with citrus mayonnaise, 98–99

I

ice cream:
cinnamon, with raspberry
sabayon and tulip shells,
235–237
hazelnut saffron, with chocolate
hazelnut sauce, 238–239

J

juniper and pheasant ravioli with
wild morel sauce, 76–78

L

lamb:
    chiffonade of, with basil pesto,
      141–142
    chops with Indian spinach sauce,
      137–138
    grilled rack of, with cumin
      coriander bordelaise, 139–140
lamb's lettuce salad with celery and
    pink peppercorn dressing, 21
lavender, sole fillets with, 100–101
lemon:
    Parmesan vinaigrette, baby
      lettuces with, 20
    tart with raspberry sauce,
      228–229
lentils, confit of duck legs and,
    64–65
lettuce(s):
    baby, with lemon Parmesan
      vinaigrette, 20
    Bibb, fresh herb cheese with
      endive and, 28–29
    Creole tomato salad, 27
    Windsor Court salad with sauce
      Lorenzo, 17–18
linguine with feta, pancetta, and
    baby artichokes, 79–80
liver(s):
    chicken and goose, terrine of,
      with Cumberland sauce, 61–63
    grilled foie gras and pears, 59–60
lobster:
    peppered, scrambled eggs with,
      195–196
    poached in honey water with
      citrus mayonnaise, 98–99
    quenelles of seafood with
      tarragon cream sauce, 49–50
    rillettes of avocado and, with
      cilantro yogurt sauce, 42–43

    sauce, 178–179
    ziti with duck, cream, and,
      70–71

M

Marsala sauce, 146
    roulade of veal with spinach,
      pine nuts, and crabmeat, and,
      145–146
mayonnaise, citrus, 99
meats:
    chiffonade of lamb with basil
      pesto, 141–142
    grilled rack of lamb with cumin
      coriander bordelaise, 139–140
    grilled veal chops with Billy's
      mother's caponata relish,
      143–144
    lamb chops with Indian spinach
      sauce, 137–138
    roulade of veal with spinach,
      pine nuts, and crabmeat, and
      Marsala sauce, 145–146
    see also beef
melon sorbet, 243–244
mint-Tabasco compound butter, 184
monkey hill, 222–223
mousse, dessert:
    chocolate breathless, 224–225
    monkey hill, 222–223
mousse, savory:
    fish, 93
    watercress, roasted salmon with,
      86–87
muffins:
    berry-nut, 207
    bran, 206
mushroom(s):
    eggs Windsor Court, 193–194
    shiitake, tuna with two sesames,
      wasabi beurre blanc, and, 94–95

soufflé, quick, 164–165
   wild morel, sauce, pheasant and
     juniper ravioli with, 76–78
mushroom(s), chanterelle:
   Folsom, sautéed snails with,
     53–54
   medallions of venison with,
     133–134
   quick mushroom soufflé,
     164–165
   and tomato soup, 11–12
mustard:
   champagne sauce, fried frog's
     legs with, 55–56
   glaze, Chinese, salmon with,
     83

N

nut(s):
   berry muffins, 207
   cashew-breaded duck breasts
     with peanut sauce,
     115–116
   shredded spinach salad with
     creamy vinaigrette and
     sugared toasted almonds,
     22–23
   see also hazelnut; pecan(s); pine
     nuts

O

omelette Linley, 197–198
onion, red, confiture, 181
orange:
   burnt, frozen soufflé, 218–219
   Chinese lacquered duck with
     coffee mandarin glaze,
     109–110
oyster-artichoke soup, 5
oysters polo, 38–39

P

pain Perdu, 199–200
pancetta, linguine with feta, baby
   artichokes, and, 79–80
Parmesan:
   basil pesto, 142
   -battered tomatoes, 159
   lemon vinaigrette, baby lettuces
     with, 20
   omelette Linley, 197–198
passion fruit sorbet, 243
pasta:
   dough, 69
   linguine with feta, pancetta, and
     baby artichokes, 79–80
   pheasant and juniper ravioli
     with wild morel sauce,
     76–78
   shrimp spaetzle with basil
     crabmeat sauce, 74–75
   sugarcane, with crawfish and
     shrimp stuffing, 72–73
   ziti with lobster, duck, and
     cream, 70–71
Pastis, fresh berries in champagne
   and, 205
peanut sauce, cashew-breaded duck
   breasts with, 115–116
pears, grilled foie gras and,
   59–60
pecan(s):
   berry muffins, 207
   squares, 230–231
   traditional New Orleans pralines,
     215
pepper(s), bell:
   Creole ratatouille, 160
   stuffed squash blossoms,
     161–162
   tri-color relish, 187
pepper, Windsor Court, 189

peppercorn(s):
  green, sauce, rosette of salmon
    and grouper with, 84–85
  pink, and celery dressing, lamb's
    lettuce salad with, 21
  scrambled eggs with peppered
    lobster, 195–196
Pernod:
  fresh berries in champagne and,
    205
  vinaigrette, frozen, grilled
    grouper with, 90–91
pesto, basil, chiffonade of lamb
    with, 141–142
pheasant and juniper ravioli
    with wild morel sauce,
    76–78
pilaf, cilantro and turmeric, 163
pine nuts:
  basil pesto, 142
  roulade of veal with spinach,
    crabmeat, and, and Marsala
    sauce, 145–146
port:
  coriander sauce, roasted Abita
    Springs quail with, 127–128
  Cumberland sauce, 63
  wild fowl braised with,
    131–132
potato(es):
  dauphine, Creole, 154–155
  rosemary baked, 156
  terrine, 153
praline(s):
  brûlée, 216–217
  monkey hill, 222–223
  traditional New Orleans, 215

Q

quail, roasted Abita Springs, with
    port-coriander sauce, 127–128

R

rabbit, panéed loin of, thermidor,
    129–130
raisin apple chutney, grilled tea-
    marinated duck breasts with
    duck cracklings and, 111–112
raspberry(ies):
  cats' tongues, 232–233
  fresh berries in champagne and
    Pastis, 205
  sabayon, cinnamon ice cream
    with tulip shells and, 235–237
  sauce, lemon tart with, 228–229
  sorbet, 242–243
  vinegar-seared, grilled chicken
    breasts with, 117–118
ratatouille, Creole, 160
ravioli, pheasant and juniper, with
    wild morel sauce, 76–78
redfish, smoked, with cucumber
    jam, 51–52
relish:
  caponata, Billy's mother's, 144
  tomato-caper, 186
  tri-color, 187
rosemary baked potatoes, 156

S

sabayon, raspberry, cinnamon ice
    cream with tulip shells and,
    235–237
saffron hazelnut ice cream with
    chocolate hazelnut sauce,
    238–239
salad dressings:
  celery and pink peppercorn, 21
  creamy vinaigrette, 23
  Creole tomato, 27
  hot crabmeat, 19
  lemon Parmesan vinaigrette, 20
  sauce Lorenzo, 17–18

salads:
  baby lettuces with lemon
    Parmesan vinaigrette, 20
  Creole tomato, 27
  cucumber, 24
  fresh herb cheese with endive
    and Bibb lettuce, 28–29
  hot crawfish with gingered
    sesame on watercress, 25–26
  lamb's lettuce, with celery and
    pink peppercorn dressing, 21
  shredded spinach, with sugared
    toasted almonds and creamy
    vinaigrette, 22–23
  spinach, with hot crabmeat
    dressing, 19
  Windsor Court, with sauce
    Lorenzo, 17–18
salmon:
  with Chinese mustard glaze, 83
  harlequin of three fish with sun-
    dried tomato sauce, 104–106
  pâté of crabmeat and, en croûte,
    46–48
  quenelles of seafood with
    tarragon cream sauce, 49–50
  roasted, with watercress mousse,
    86–87
  rosette of grouper and, with
    green peppercorn sauce, 84–85
salsa, black bean, 103
sauces:
  apple raisin chutney, 112
  basil crabmeat, 75
  béchamel, 175
  beurre blanc #1, 173
  beurre blanc #2, 174
  chocolate hazelnut, 239
  cilantro yogurt, 43
  citrus mayonnaise, 99
  clarified butter, 180
  Cumberland, 63

cumin coriander bordelaise,
  140
egg wash, 190
fresh tomato tartar, 97
garlic spread, 183
ginger, 120
hollandaise, 176–177
lobster, 178–179
Lorenzo, 17–18
Marsala, 146
peanut, 116
raspberry, 229
red onion confiture, 181
spiced glazing butter, 182
sun-dried tomato, 105
Tabasco-mint compound butter,
  184
tomato béarnaise, 194
tomato-caper relish, 186
tomatoes concassé, 185
tri-color relish, 187
wild morel, 77
see also salad dressings;
  spices
sausage, crawfish, 34–36
scallops, grilled marinated, with
  black bean salsa, 102–103
scones, currant, 208–209
sesame, gingered, hot crawfish
  with, on watercress, 25–26
sesames, two, tuna with wasabi
  beurre blanc, shiitake
  mushrooms, and, 94–95
shellfish:
  crawfish Sarah Jane, 33
  crawfish sausage, 34–36
  grilled marinated scallops with
    black bean salsa, 102–103
  hot crawfish with gingered
    sesame on watercress, 25–26
  oyster-artichoke soup, 5
  oysters polo, 38–39

shellfish (*continued*)

  potted crawfish, 37

  quenelles of seafood with
    tarragon cream sauce, 49–50

  shrimp and cilantro bisque, 3–4

  shrimp sautéed with citrus fruit,
    40–41

  shrimp spaetzle with basil
    crabmeat sauce, 74–75

  sugarcane pasta with crawfish
    and shrimp stuffing, 72–73

  see also crab(meat); lobster
    shortbread, Windsor Court
    strawberry, 213–214

shrimp:

  and cilantro bisque, 3–4

  and crawfish stuffing, sugarcane
    pasta with, 72–73

  sautéed with citrus fruit,
    40–41

  spaetzle with basil crabmeat
    sauce, 74–75

side dishes:

  cilantro and turmeric pilaf, 163

  quick mushroom soufflé,
    164–165

  see also vegetable(s)

snails, sautéed, with Folsom
  chanterelles, 53–54

snapper, red:

  quenelles of seafood with
    tarragon cream sauce, 49–50

  with vanilla, 88–89

sole:

  fillets with lavender, 100–101

  fish stock, 170

sorbet(s):

  gingered tea, 234

  Harlequin mask with trio of,
    241–244

  melon, 243–244

  passion fruit, 243

  raspberry, 242–243

soufflé, dessert:

  bourbon whiskey, 220–221

  frozen burnt orange, 218–219

soufflé, savory:

  crabmeat, 44–45

  quick mushroom, 164–165

soups:

  chanterelle and tomato, 11–12

  crab and corn, with corn fritters,
    6–7

  gazpacho with cumin, basil, and
    crabmeat, 13–14

  oyster-artichoke, 5

  shrimp and cilantro bisque, 3–4

  strawberry champagne, 10

  turtle, 8–9

soup stock, *see* stock

spaetzle, shrimp, with basil
  crabmeat sauce, 74–75

spiced glazing butter, 182

spices:

  Harvey's curry powder, 188

  Windsor Court pepper, 189

spinach:

  roulade of veal with pine nuts,
    crabmeat, and, and Marsala
    sauce, 145–146

  salad with hot crabmeat
    dressing, 19

  sauce, Indian, lamb chops with,
    137–138

  shredded, salad with sugared
    toasted almonds and creamy
    vinaigrette, 22–23

squash blossoms, stuffed,
  161–162

steak Romanoff, 66

stock:

  chicken, 169

  demi-glace, 171–172

  fish, 170

strawberry(ies):
  champagne soup, 10
  fresh berries in champagne and
    Pastis, 205
  Pontchatoula beignets with
    bourbon whiskey whipped
    cream, 201–202
  shortbread, Windsor Court,
    213–214

T

Tabasco-mint compound butter,
  184
tarragon cream sauce, quenelles of
  seafood with, 49–50
tartar sauce, fresh tomato,
  Louisiana crab cakes with,
  96–97
tea:
  -marinated duck breasts, grilled,
    with duck cracklings and apple
    raisin chutney, 111–112
  sorbet, gingered, 234
tomato(es):
  béarnaise sauce, 194
  caper relish, 186
  and chanterelle soup, 11–12
  cheese-battered, 159
  concassé, 185
  Creole ratatouille, 160
  fresh, tartar sauce, Louisiana
    crab cakes with, 96–97
  gazpacho with cumin, basil, and
    crabmeat, 13–14
  salad, Creole, 27
  stuffed squash blossoms,
    161–162
  sun-dried, sauce, harlequin of
    three fish with, 104–106
truffles, chocolate, 240
tulip shells, cinnamon ice cream

with raspberry sabayon and,
  235–237
tuna:
  harlequin of three fish with sun-
    dried tomato sauce, 104–106
  with two sesames, wasabi beurre
    blanc, and shiitake
    mushrooms, 94–95
turkey breast, stuffed, with roast
  gravy, 123–124
turmeric and cilantro pilaf,
  163
turtle soup, 8–9

V

veal:
  chops, grilled, with Billy's
    mother's caponata relish,
    143–144
  demi-glace, 171–172
  mock turtle soup, 8–9
  roulade of, with spinach,
    pine nuts, and crabmeat,
    and Marsala sauce,
    145–146
vegetable(s):
  cheese-battered tomatoes,
    159
  Creole potatoes dauphine,
    154–155
  Creole ratatouille, 160
  potato terrine, 153
  rosemary baked potatoes, 156
  stuffed squash blossoms,
    161–162
  terrine, 157–158
venison, medallions of, with
  chanterelles, 133–134
vinaigrette:
  dressing, creamy, 23
  frozen Pernod, 90

vinaigrette (*continued*)
   lemon Parmesan, 20

W

walnut-berry muffins, 207
watercress:
   hot crawfish with gingered
      sesame on, 25–26
   mousse, roasted with 86–87
   Windsor Court salad with sauce
      Lorenzo, 17–18
whipped cream:
   bourbon whiskey, Pontchatoula
      beignets with, 201–202

Windsor Court strawberry
   shortbread, 213–214

Y

yogurt sauce, cilantro, rillettes of
   lobster, and avocado with,
   42–43

Z

ziti with lobster, duck, and cream,
   70–71